From The Healing Foods Series:

CW01095747

Healing Herbs & Spices
Health Benefits of Popular Herbs & Spices Plus Over 70 Recipes To Use Them In

Table Of Contents

The information included in this book is for educational purposes only and is not meant to be a substitute for seeking the advice of a health care professional. This information is not meant to replace modern medicines or medical treatments. The author and publisher make no claims as to the ability of the herbs and spices listed in this book to cure or treat you of any ailment known to man. Before using and herbs or spices, you should consult your doctor.

The author and publisher has made their best efforts to ensure the information in this book is accurate, however, they make no warranties as the accuracy or completeness of the contents herein and cannot be held responsible for any errors, omissions or dated material. The information given in this book may not be suitable for your situation and you should consult a professional before trying any remedies or recipes listed in this book. The publisher and author assume no responsibility for any outcome resulting in applying the information found in this book, either through self care or under the care of a health care professional. Neither the publisher or author shall be liable for any damages including but not limited to special, incidental, consequential or other damages. If you have health concerns, talk to a qualified professional first.

Dedication

This book is dedicated to my mother in law Mildred "Mod" Dowse because she introduced me to the healing benefits of food. I hope I can be as active, vivacious and healthy as you are!

Introduction

I'd never been introduced to herbs or spices in my youth, so it seems odd that I would be writing a book about them now, much less one loaded with recipes!

My mother never really used spices, I think she might have had some oregano and maybe some cinnamon in the back of the cabinet but even those were rarely used. My childhood comfort foods were mostly meat and potato dishes with very little zip in the way of spices but still delicious and comforting.

Up until I was in my mid 30's I had no idea that what you ate could affect your health. It wasn't until my mother-in-law lent me the book "Fit For Life" by Harvey & Marilyn Diamond that I realized the profound affect foods could have on you. Reading that book started a life long journey into learning about food, herbs and spices and how to use them for health and cooking.

This book includes some of the more popular herbs and spices in use today. Inside you will find out how important these can be to your health and I hope you will realize, like I did, that adding them to your everyday cooking can greatly affect the way you feel both mentally and physically.

This isn't a book about healthy eating though, I wrote it so that you could be aware of how some of these everyday herbs and spices can improve your health and included the recipes as a way for you to see how you can easily get more of them into your diet.

Although many of the recipes are "healthy" for you, I have also included some of my favorites that probably aren't so healthy but are still a good way to add these healing herbs and spices to your diet.

I hope you enjoy this book and I hope that you will leave me a review on Amazon to let me know what you think. I'm interested in the good and the bad and I really appreciate you taking the time to leave one!

To your health!

Lee Anne Dobbins

Preface

If it wasn't for herbs and spices, the new world might never have been discovered.

We take them for granted now, but back in the 1400's spices were a big deal. Most of the expeditions revolved around bringing spices back to Europe where they were quite expensive and highly sought after.

Europe didn't really have any spices that grew natively so most of the spices were imported from Africa and Asia. The Venetian Republic in Italy had a monopoly on the spice trade. As you can imagine, there was a lot of money in spices so finding new trade routes was highly desirable for all European countries and this is actually what Columbus was after when he "discovered" America.

Spices have been used since 50,000 BC and have been connected with magic, medicine, religion, preservation and, of course, flavoring food. While they aren't as coveted or expensive as they once were, spices still play an important role in many cultures today in both the areas of healing and cooking.

Herbs & Spices and Your Health

Once you take a good look at the health benefits of herbs and spices you'll see that it's no accident that they are traditionally included in most dishes because most of the herbs and spices help with various digestive issues in addition to other health problems.

As you probably already know, herbs and spices have been used since ancient times for medicinal purposes and they are reputed to be able to help heal everything from bee stings to gout to cancer. In fact, many of the medicines we have today are based on compounds found in these herbs.

Sadly, there have not been a lot of clinical trials to study the effects of herbs on various illnesses so there isn't a lot of proof out there as to whether these work well or not. The healing benefits listed in this book come from common knowledge of ancient healing but, when I could find it, I have listed studies from modern medicine which help support these healthy benefits.

Most herbs and spices are perfectly safe to use in food amounts so there's no reason not to try to get more of them by using them more in your cooking. If you focus on certain herbs and spices that are reputed to heal health problems that you are experiencing, you just might find your health improving. That being said, some herbs and spices can have an adverse effect on medicines you may be taking or on illnesses you may currently have, so you will want to consult with your doctor before you add any new herbs or spices into your diet.

Herbs & Spices and Your Cooking

Herbs and spices add zip to your food and, without them, most dishes would be bland and flavorless. There are many ways to use them and lots of spices come in dried form for convenience but you will find that using them fresh is usually preferred because that's where you'll get the most flavor as well as health benefits.

In this book I've listed 80 of the most popular herbs and spices that you might want to consider including as part of your culinary regimen. You will find that most of the recipes include more than one spice, so you will be able to get a variety of spices in each meal quite easily.

Of course, there are many more spices and herbs to be explored than listed in this book. I've only included the most common ones. Ones that you can find easily and won't have to make trips to a specialty store for. These are the ones that you will use most of all. But if you get bored with these, you can always branch out and explore to find more wonderful herbs and spices you can use for cooking and healing.

Now, onto the spices and herbs!

ALLSPICE

Plant Family: Myrtle (Myrtaceae)

Where Grown: Jamaica, Caribbean, South America

Parts Used: Berries mostly, sometimes the leaves

Other Names: Pimento, Jamaica pepper, Myrtle Pepper, Clove pepper

I used to think that allspice was actually a combination of all spices. Of course, that was before I knew there were way too many spices to combine them all in one small jar or that doing so would be a culinary nightmare. If I'd bothered to look at the actual spice itself I would have known right off that I was wrong, because allspice is a dried berry.

Native to the Caribbean, allspice is the fruit of an evergreen plant called Pimento officinalis or Pimento diocia that can grow to heights of 40 feet. These brown berries are round and a bit larger than peppercorns. They are used dried and have a peppery bite, a taste reminiscent of cloves but a bit lighter and with some cinnamon and juniper thrown in for good measure.

The best quality allspice comes from Jamaica where berries are harvested before they ripen and dried to a leathery brown in the hot Caribbean sun. When buying allspice, make sure that the berries are not broken or dusty looking. Don't buy the powder version as, while this may seem convenient to have them already ground, the mixture will likely contain other powders in addition to the allspice.

Store the berries in a tightly sealed container at room temperature and mill them with a hand mill as required. They should keep for several years in berry form.

Health Benefits

Allspice is mostly thought of as a culinary herb, but it also has some healing properties you might want to explore. Like most herbs, this little berry has oils and that's where most of the magic happens. The oil contains a compound called eugenol which is said to have pain relieving, antiseptic and anti bacterial properties.

In fact, dentists use this oil as a anesthetic and it is an ingredient found in some topical products for sensitive gums including Numizident and Benzoden.

One should be careful when using the essential oils though as it can have adverse effects if ingested.

Much safer, is the powder made from grinding the allspice berry. It is said to help activate digestive enzymes which aids in digestion as well as relive gas and bloating. The best way to take it is in a tea - combine 1 or 2 teaspoons of powder in a cup of boiling water and steep for 10 minutes. Drink up to 3 of these a day to alleviate digestive problems.

Allspice has also been used traditionally as a remedy for muscle ache. Just grind up the allspice and mix it with water to make a paste. Make a poultice and apply directly to the area.

This spice also has antioxidant properties and contains some essential vitamins and minerals such as iron magnesium, potassium, copper, selenium, vitamin A, vitamin B6, Vitamin C, riboflavin and niacin.

Side Effects: This spice is on the FDA's list of herbs that are safe for external use. Be sure to use the oil sparingly - only 1 or two drops topically and do not ingest it as it can result in eugenol poisoning which may cause nausea and even convulsions. The powder is safe to use however, although some people might be allergic to allspice. When used topically it could cause rash or inflammation if you have sensitive skin. Individuals with stomach ulcers, ulcerative colitis, and diverticulitis should avoid eating dishes made with this spice. As always, consult your doctor before consuming any new food or if you have any questions or adverse reactions.

Culinary Uses

When using allspice in cooking, you want to grind the berry right before you use it. This will insure you get the best flavor from the spice. Allspice should be added to the dish at the final stages of cooking so as to limit evaporation of the flavorful essential oils.

Allspice is used quite a bit in Caribbean cuisines and dishes like curries, jerk seasonings and even some liqueurs. In the west it is associated more with things like mulled cider and holiday foods.

Jamaican Jerk Seasoning

Use this seasoning as a rub on chicken, pork or beef.
Marinate overnight and then grill the meat as usual.

Ingredients:

• 1/2 cup allspice powder made from freshly ground
berries
• 1/2 cup packed dark brown sugar
• 4 - 6 Scotch Bonnet Peppers seeded and cored
• 1 teaspoon cinnamon
• 1/2 teaspoon nutmeg
• 8 cloves of garlic
• 1 tablespoon thyme ground up
• 2 bunches scallions cut up small
• Salt and pepper to taste
• Enough soy sauce to moisten it (about 2 tablespoons)

Preparation:

Place all the ingredients in a food processor or blender and
blend until mixed. Use as a rub on your favorite meat. Let
the meat marinate overnight.

Healthy Banana Spice Muffins

Ingredients:

- 1/2 teaspoon ground nutmeg
- 1/8 teaspoon ground allspice
- 1 cup all-purpose flour
- 1 cup whole wheat flour
- 1/2 cup granulated sugar (or 1/4 cup granulated sugar and 1/4 cup agave nectar)
- 2 teaspoons baking powder
- 1/2 teaspoon baking soda
- 1/8 teaspoon salt
- 1 egg
- 1/3 cup oil
- 1/2 cup buttermilk
- 1/2 cup mashed bananas, very ripe (use ones that are mostly brown on the outside)

Preparation:

Spray muffin pans with nonstick spray or use muffin cups

Preheat oven to 400 degrees F.

Combine the dry ingredients - allspice, nutmeg, salt, baking powder and soda, whole wheat flour, regular flour and sugar - in a large bowl. Mix well.

Combine the wet ingredients - banana, oil and buttermilk. Mix well.

Add the wet ingredients into the dry ingredients stirring lightly until they are just blended together.

Fill the muffin cups 2/3 full and bake at 400 degrees F for about 20 minutes until they are golden brown in color. Insert a toothpick in the middle and if it comes out clean, you know they are done!

ANISE

Plant Family: Parsley (Umbellifarae)

Where Grown: Mediterranean, Egypt, Turkey

Parts Used: Seeds

Other Names: Aniseed, White Anise

I grew up in an Italian family and one of my favorite childhood memories is of eating delicate pizzelle cookies - the thin waffle shaped cookie with the sweet licorice taste of anise.   You might recognize the seeds of those that cling to biscotti, another Italian cookie, that you often see on display in glass jars in coffee shops.

But it's not just the Italians that love this sweet seed, the Greeks use it to make the popular liqueur Ouzo, the French put them in stews and in India these seeds, along with their cousins fennel and cumin, are coated in sugar and served after a meal to aid in digestion and freshen breath.

Anise is a herbaceous plant that grows about 3 feet tall and yields white flowers. Sometimes the leaves are used but that is rare and it is mostly the small seeds that from this plant that are used. It is native to the Mediterranean but can grow most anywhere.

Most commonly we find brown or white anise but there is another variation with black seeds (called, appropriately enough, black anise) which is rarely found and much coveted as it produces a much sweeter seed. Don't confuse either one of these with star anise which is a totally different plant and has a   more peppery taste.

Seeds that are fresh are best to use in cooking. Store your anise seeds in a cool, dry place inside a glass container with a tight fitting lid.

Health Benefits

Anise seeds have been used for healing for centuries and are referenced in Egyptian, Chinese and Indian culture.

Anise seed has been used to help alleviate coughing and the phytochemicals in the seed have powerful antiseptic properties and also help act as an expectorant. It's long been associated with relief from colds as evidenced by the licorice taste of cough drops. Anise can also help alleviate symptoms of asthma.

It can also help alleviate gas and digestive problems. Chewing on the seeds can act as a natural "Tums" and it's a bit more tasty too! Take them to relieve bad breath, nausea, bloating, gas and indigestion.

Another compound in anise is anethol, which has estrogenic properties and can help alleviate menstrual problems as well as help nursing mothers produce more breast milk.

Anise oil, when applied topically, can help alleviate oily skin and acne. It is also reputed to be a good way to get rid of scabies and kill lice.

Texts from ancient Egypt show it being used as an herbal diuretic and the ancient Greek Dioscorides write that it "warms, dries and dissolves" many symptoms and also that it "provokes urine, facilitates breathing, relieves pain and eases thirst". Even Hippocrates knew of this flavorful little seed and suggested it to control coughing.

Use the seeds in a tea combining 2 teaspoon of crushed seeds with 1 cup boiling water. Let steep for 10 minutes than drink up! Take up to 3 cups a day.

Anise seeds are loaded with B complex vitamins like niacin, pyridoxine, riboflavin, and thiamin a well as Vitamin A and Vitamin C. It also contains the minerals calcium, phosphorus, potassium, sulphur, iron, manganese, magnesium, copper and zinc.

Side Effects: As with any essential oil, one must use anise oil with caution as it can be toxic. The seeds do not contain much oil though and can be used in doses as specified above. Pregnant women should avoid anise (other than as a mild spice in cooking) as it does contain anethol.

Culinary Uses

With it's sweet licorice taste, anise seeds are quite popular in many dessert dishes but it is also uses in stews, breads and curries too. It can even go well with eggs, cheeses and many vegetable dishes.

As with most seeds, the flavor is in the oils which only come out when the seed is crushed. To get the most flavor, you will want to store the seeds whole and crush or grind them just before using in your dish.

Pizzelle Cookies

Ingredients:

- 1/2 teaspoon ground anise seeds
- 1 teaspoon vanilla
- 3 eggs
- 1/2 cups butter, melted (cooled)
- 3/4 cups sugar
- 1 3/4 cups flour
- 2 teaspoons baking powder

Preparation:

Beat the eggs and sugar together.

Stir in the cooled, melted butter, vanilla and anise seeds.

Sift together the baking powder and flour, mixing well.

Add the flour mixture to the egg mixture and mix well.

Cook, following the instructions on your pizzelle maker.

Anise Squash Soup

Ingredients:

- 1 teaspoon anise seeds, toasted
- 1 tablespoon olive oil
- 2 medium onions, chopped
- 1 teaspoon salt
- 2 Pounds squash cut into 1" chunks
- 1 pint vegetable stock
- 1–2 cups skim milk

Preparation:

Heat olive oil in a large skillet.

Add onions and salt to the skillet and sauté until onions are translucent.

Add squash and anise seeds to skillet and cook until squash is soft, stirring frequently to get all the brown bits up from the bottom and into your mixture.

Add vegetable stock and simmer for 15 minutes.

Transfer the contents of the skillet to a blender and add 1/4 of the skim milk. Puree the entire mixture adding more milk until it is creamy but not too liquid (you may not need to use all the milk).

BASIL

Plant Family: Mint (Lamiaceae)

Where Grown: Originally from India but can grow anywhere

Parts Used: Leaves

Other Names: Sweet basil

I always associate basil with Italian cooking, but the truth is that this aromatic herb originated in India. It is, perhaps, the Italians that have made it famous though as it is such a staple ingredient in most Italian dishes and the base for pesto sauce.

Basil has a sweet peppery taste, almost like a combination of mint and oregano. It can vary quite a bit in its flavors with some versions being more minty and some more peppery depending on the soil conditions of where it is grown.

Basil is one of the most popular kitchen herbs and there are a lot of hybrids all with different leaf sizes, colors and flavors from lemon to anise. It's quite easy to grow right on your windowsill and can be found fresh in most grocery stores today either already picked or growing in pots already for you, so there is no excuse to use the dried version - with basil fresh is best!

I highly suggest you pick up a plant and set it on your windowsill. It looks great and smells great too. Just pinch off a leaf or two depending on what you need in your recipe and I guarantee you will be hooked on always having a basil plant around.

If you don't take my advice, the fresh basil found in bunches in the grocery store can be stored in the fridge for 3 or 4 days or frozen. The dried version of this herb won't be nearly as good as the fresh or frozen.

Health Benefits

Basil has many healing properties but perhaps its biggest benefit has to do with its antibacterial properties. In fact, a study done in July 2003 and published in the Journal of Microbiology Methods found that basil's essential oil inhibited bacteria such as Staphylococcus, Pseudomonas and Enterococcus. These are all common bacteria that have built up a resistance to being treated with antibiotics.

It also contains many anti-inflammatory oils such as eugenol, citronellol, limonene and terpineol. Eugenol specifically is thought to help alleviate inflammation due to arthritis and inflammatory bowel condition.

Basil can also be used topically to alleviate insect bites and stings. Just crush the leaves and rub it on the affected area.

Basil tea can help relax you, may help with insomnia as well as alleviate painful menstruation symptoms. To make a tea, shred up 2 tablespoons of basil leaves and add to 1 cup of boiling water. Let it steep for 5 minutes. Drink 3 cups a day preferably after each meal. This can also help treat diarrhea and urinary tract infections.

Basil is an excellent source of Vitamin K and also contains iron, calcium, Vitamin A, manganese, magnesium, Vitamin C and potassium.

Culinary Uses

As mentioned above, you should always use basil fresh as the dried herb loses a lot of its sweet flavor. In cooking, Basil should be added just before bringing the dish to the table. Tearing or crushing the leaves (instead of chopping) will help to release its sweet flavor.

Basil is used in all types of cuisine from Italian pasta dishes to French soups to Thai food to Mediterranean stews. It's perfect for salads and my favorite is a simple Caprese salad made of basil, tomato and mozzarella drizzled with a little olive oil. Perhaps the most famous culinary use of basil is the Italian pesto sauce which combines basil, oil, pine nuts, garlic and parmesan cheese.

Basil Pesto

Ingredients:

- 2 cups basil leaves
- 1/2 cup olive oil
- 1/3 cup pine nuts (pignolis)
- 1/2 cup parmesan cheese, freshly grated
- 3-4 cloves of garlic chopped

Preparation:

Pulse the basil, pine nuts and garlic in a food processor about 10 seconds - just until mixed.

Turn the food processor on slow and pour in the olive oil in through the feed tube while the processor is processing. You can scrape down the sides as needed to insure everything gets mixed. Keep processing until the ingredients are mixed into a puree.

Add the grated cheese at the end and pulse a few times to mix.

Salt and pepper to taste.

Basil Syrup

This can be used to drizzle over fruit salad or regular salad or to use as a starter for a refreshing summer drink. To make a drink combine 2 cups of the syrup with 2 cups of water, ice cubes and a teaspoon lemon or orange zest.

Ingredients:

- 3 cups packed basil leaves shredded
- 3 cups sugar
- 3 cups water

Preparation:

Combine sugar and water in saucepan and bring to a boil while stirring.

Keep on heat and stir until sugar is dissolved.

Remove from heat and add basil leaves stirring well.

Let the mixture cool to room temperature and strain.

Store in an airtight container in fridge for 5 days or freeze.

Basil Chicken

Ingredients:

- 1/2 cup fresh basil leaves shredded
- 1/8 teaspoon salt
- 2 teaspoons olive oil
- 1 large sweet onion chopped
- 1 clove garlic chopped
- 2 cups tomatoes chopped
- 2 cups chicken breast meat cut into 1" cubes
- 1/2 cup parmesan cheese

Preparation:

In a large skillet, sauté oil, garlic and onions.

Stir in salt chicken and tomato.

Cover and reduce heat allowing the mixture to simmer for about 5 minutes until tomatoes are soft. Stir frequently.

Remove from heat and stir in basil leaves until well mixed.

Serve this delicious dish over pasta or lay it on a bed of greens for a low carb meal.

BAY LEAF (Turkish)

Plant Family: Laurel (Lauraceae)
Where Grown: Turkey, Mediterranean, Egypt

Parts Used: Leaves

Other Names: Bay Laurel, Poet's Laurel, Sweet Bay, Roman Laurel

There are actually several varieties of bay leaf, but the dried leaves from the Turkish bay laurel are the ones found in most kitchens and the ones that have found their way into countless soups and stews.

There's no mistaking the camphor like pine scent of these leaves and the best ones will have a strong scent. This herb is used dried because the fresh leaves have little flavor. It is only after several weeks of drying in the shade that full flavor is developed. The leaves should be whole and green in color - not brownish.

Although they aren't really that pleasant to eat, it is an old wives tale that you will fall ill if you consume them.

The plant these leaves come from is an evergreen which sports white flowers that turn to greenish purple berries. The leaves are what is mainly used both for healing and cooking and these are tough, thick leaves that are shiny and about 3 inches in length.

You will find the leaves whole in the store, usually sitting up right in a glass container. They will keep for about a year if stored in a dark, dry spot.

Health Benefits

The ancient Greeks and Romans loved this herb and even went so far as to make crowns out of it by intertwining the leaves. The medicinal properties of this leaf are well known and it has diuretic as well as astringent properties and is said to help stimulate appetite.

The lauric acid contained in the leaf can act as an insect repellent and, in fact these leaves were used to keep moths away in ancient times.

Bay leaves have many uses when it comes to healing. Like most herbs, the oils contained in it have anti bacterial, anti fungal and anti inflammatory properties that can help treat a host of ills. In particular the parthenolides contained in bay leaf can be used to treat headaches and has been proven useful in treating migraines. These pungent leaves are also said to help normalize blood sugar by aiding the body in processing insulin efficiently.

One of the biggest uses for this leaf is to soothe the stomach and relieve flatulence. It can also act as a mild sedative so including it in a tea before bedtime could be helpful if you are having trouble sleeping.

Bay leaves are a good source of Vitamin C, folic acid, Vitamin A, niacin, pyridoxine, pantothenic acid, riboflavin, copper, potassium, calcium, manganese, iron, selenium, zing and magnesium.

Side Effects: Bay leaf is relatively safe when eaten in the normal amounts you use in food. Contact with it can cause dermatitis and even eczema in some individuals. It may cause occupational asthma. Be warned, the leaves are extremely tough and sharp and cannot be digested as they could become lodged in the digestive tract causing tears or even a blockage. Best not to eat the leaves unless chopped up in to small pieces. It is advised to not eat too much of this before you are having surgery.

Culinary Uses

Bay leaves are used mainly to flavor dishes and not necessarily to be eaten in the dish. Since the leaves themselves have a bitter taste, are very tough and cannot be digested, it is recommended you remove it from the dish after cooking.

This is one of the few herbs that should be included into the dish before cooking as it imparts its best flavors as it cooks. Bay leaves should simmer for 20 minutes or more to release all the savory goodness.

Bay leaves are commonly used in soup stock, stews, fish and meat dishes, marinades, vegetable dishes and bouillabaisse.

Bay Leaf And Garlic Rice

Ingredients:

- 3 Turkish bay leaves
- 1 clove garlic minced
- 1 tablespoon olive oil
- 1 3/4 cups reduced sodium chicken broth or chicken stock
- 1 1/4 cups rice
- 1/4 teaspoon salt
- 1/4 teaspoon pepper

Preparation:

Sauté by leaves and oil in a large saucepan over medium low heat until leaves are browned.

Add garlic and sauté until golden.

Add salt, pepper and rice - stir for about 1 minute.

Add chicken broth, turn heat to high and bring to a boil.

Cover with a lid and reduce heat to low.

Simmer until the rice has absorbed the liquid - about 15 or 20 minutes.

*Remove bay leaves before serving!

Potato Bay Leaf Bake

Ingredients:

- 5 bay leaves
- 3 pounds potatoes cut into 1/2" slices
- 3 cloves garlic chopped
- 3 cups chicken stock
- 3 tablespoons olive oil
- Salt and pepper to taste

Preparation:

Brush a large deep skillet with 1 tablespoon olive oil.

Layer potatoes, garlic and bay leaves on the bottom of the skillet.

Drizzle remaining olive oil over the layer.

Make a second layer of the remaining potatoes garlic and bay leaves.

Pour the chicken stock over the top.

Cook on high until it comes to a boil.

Cover and reduce heat to simmer for 30 minutes.

Remove the remaining liquid as well as the bay leaves and enjoy!

CARAWAY

Plant Family: Parsley (Umbelliferae)

Where Grown: Northern Europe, Asia, Canada, Russia, Netherlands

Parts Used: Fruit (most people think they are seeds)

Other Names: Roman cumin

If you like rye bread then you'll be quite familiar with this little tasty seed-like fruit that comes from a biennial plant which can be grown most anywhere and is native to Europe. Standing 2 feet tall, the plant produces white flowers and the "seeds" which are long and ridged are actually fruit. It is this fruit that is used for cooking and healing.

Caraway has a pungent flavor reminiscent of licorice but not overly sweet. It tastes a lot like cumin which is why it is often called Roman cumin.

Caraway has been used since the middle ages in breads and cakes and also as a digestive aid. It is thought that it might even be the oldest spice used in Europe. Today it can be grown most anywhere but is chiefly produced in Holland.

Like most seeds, caraway should be purchased whole and then ground just before use to insure freshness. Store in a tightly sealed container in a cool, dark, dry place and the seeds should keep for months.

Health Benefits

Caraway is said to be one of the strongest carminative herbs (carminative herbs help alleviate gastrointestinal problems) and is used for relief of gas, intestinal pain and even bowel spasms. In addition to your usual stomach complaints, caraway can also be effective in ridding the body of internal parasites like hookworm.

These seeds also are loaded with fiber - 38 g for each 100 g of seeds. The increased bulk that is added with this fiber allows food to move quickly through your intestines and also binds to toxins which help protect the colon.

Caraway can also be used to alleviate bad breath - just chew a few seeds at the end of a meal or when needed. It is also rumored that chewing caraway seeds can help hide the smell of alcohol on your breath.

Caraway may also be effective in treating sore throat, cough, fever, colds, liver problems, and gallbladder problems.

Caraway seeds have lots of minerals and vitamins including Vitamin A, Vitamin E, B complex vitamins, Vitamin C, iron, calcium, copper, selenium, zinc, magnesium and manganese.

Caraway can be used as an effective treatment for digestive disorders in tea form. Combine 2 teaspoons of pressed or ground seeds with 1 cup boiling water and steep for 10 minutes. Filter out the seeds and drink the tea. 1 to 3 cups a day is recommended.

Side Effects: Caraway seeds themselves have few side effects. If you eat a lot of them, they may cause heartburn. Caraway essential oils should be used with caution on children and avoided by pregnant women.

Culinary Uses

Caraway can be used in both sweet and savory dishes and is commonly used in Indian, Russian, Scandinavian, German and Indonesian cooking. It is commonly used in breads as well as cheeses.

When cooking with caraway make sure to add the seeds towards the end of the cooking process. You don't want to cook them for much more than 15 minute or they can turn bitter. Grinding the seeds right before adding them will give more flavor to your dish.

Lemon Caraway Broccoli

Ingredients:

- 1 teaspoon caraway seeds
- 1 head of broccoli
- 1/2 teaspoon grated lemon rind
- 1 tablespoon olive oil

Preparation:

Steam broccoli until tender - about 5 minutes. Drain.

Put broccoli on serving dish, drizzle the olive oil over the top

Combine lemon rind, and caraway seeds and sprinkle over the top.

Herbed Cheese Ball

Ingredients:

- 16 oz cream cheese
- 1 cup shredded cheddar cheese
- 1 teaspoon caraway seeds
- 1 teaspoon basil (dried or chopped very fine)
- 1 teaspoon dill seed
- 2 teaspoons chopped fresh chives
- 1/8 teaspoon salt
- 1/8 teaspoon pepper
- 1/2 cup pecans or walnuts finely chopped

Preparation:

Combine cream cheese and cheddar cheese in a bowl until well mixed.

Add the rest of the ingredients except the chopped nuts and form into a round ball.

Roll the cheese ball in the chopped nuts to coat the outside.

Refrigerate overnight.

CARDAMOM

Plant Family: Ginger (Zingiberaceae)

Where Grown: India, Guatemala

Parts Used: Seeds and seed pods

Other Names: Green cardamom

Cardamom's seed pods open to reveal black seeds held together by a membrane. They have a little bit of heat to them and taste a bit like allspice, clove and sassafras all combined into a peppery explosion of flavor and camphor undertones.

Cardamom is one of the ancient spices originating from India and grown in many places today. It is used to flavor all kinds of foods and drink as well as for medicine. Ancient Greeks used it as perfume and Egyptians chewed it as a tooth cleaner.

Cardamom is the second most expensive spice (Saffron being the most expensive) and there are two different varieties you might come across. The black cardamom (which is really brown in color) and green cardamom (shown above) which is a bit smaller and green. Green cardamom is more expensive, higher quality, and preferable for both cooking and medicinal purposes.

You should buy the seed pods whole as cardamom will soon lose its flavor once crushed open. Avoid decorticated cardamom which is just the seeds as they will not be very flavorful.

Health Benefits

Cardamom has great overall detoxifying and revitalizing properties. It can help ease digestive problems and can also act as a stimulant.

Chewing the seeds is said to help remedy headaches as well as nausea, stomach pain and phlegm. A study in the 1960's showed that a volatile oil linked to the seed acts as an effective antispasmodic and could help treat gas pain, colic and cramps. It has been used as a tooth cleaner and breath freshener since ancient times.

One of the main chemicals in cardamom is cineole which acts as an expectorant. Therefore, cardamom can be effective in treating coughs and easing lung related problems such as bronchitis and asthma. It may also be effective in treating sinus congestion.

It is said to be great at detoxifying the body and has been used as a tonic in many countries.

Cardamom is relatively safe when used in foods. However, if you have gallstones you should avoid cardamom. A tincture made from this herb is subject to legal restrictions in some countries.

Culinary Uses

Cardamom can be used in both sweet and savory dishes. Either way, you want to store the seed pods whole in air tight containers and then crush the seed pods to reveal the seeds just before cooking. Cardamom will lose its flavor quickly so you want to use the seeds right away once they are out of the pod.

Cardamom is used by many cultures. In Scandinavian countries they use it in baking, in the Arab world they use it to flavor coffee and in India you will find it present in many curries.

Cardamom seeds can make a great addition to most any food and can be added to rice, custard, and pudding as well as for flavoring fruits or fruit salad. The seed pods can be added whole to soups and stews for a wonderful flavor.

Ground cardamom is what most people are used to using for baking. The powder found in the stores will not be as flavorful as the seeds so you will want to grind your own seeds with a mortar and pestle or grinder (some people grind the pod right in with the seeds) and use this for your recipe. Make sure you grind it down to a fine powder especially for baking as you don't want any cardamom lumps in your baked goods - biting into one would not be very pleasant because the flavor would be too strong.

Cardamom Bread Pudding

Ingredients:

- 1 1/2 teaspoons ground cardamom
- 1 teaspoon vanilla extract
- 3/4 teaspoon ground cinnamon
- 1/2 teaspoon ground nutmeg
- 1 cup brown sugar
- 1/2 cup white sugar
- 3 eggs
- 1/2 cup butter, melted
- 1 1/2 cups milk
- 1/2 cup cream
- 1/2 teaspoon salt
- 1 loaf of challah bread or white bread cut into cubes and crust removed

Preparation:

Preheat oven to 350F.

Grease a 9x13 baking dish.

Mix cardamom, vanilla, cinnamon, nutmeg, brown sugar, white sugar, eggs, butter, milk, cream and salt in a bowl.

Place the bread cubes into the baking dish evenly.

Pour the wet mixture over the bread cubes.

Cover and refrigerate until the bread has absorbed most of the liquid (about 30 minutes).

Uncover and put in the oven. Bake at 350F for 45 minutes.

Cardamom Chicken Stew

Ingredients:

- 1 large onion diced
- 1/4 cup butter
- Pinch salt
- 1/4 teaspoon ground cardamom
- 1/4 teaspoon black pepper
- 2 cloves garlic minced
- 2 cloves
- 1 1/2 tablespoon chopped ginger
- 1 tablespoon chili powder
- 2 1/2 cups chicken stock
- 1/4 cup dry red wine
- 2 chicken legs
- 2 chicken thighs
- 2 chicken breasts

Preparation:

In a large stew pot, melt half the butter.

Sauté onions and a pinch of salt in the butter for 10 minutes.

Add the rest of the butter, cardamom, pepper, garlic, cloves and ginger to the pot and cook another 10 minutes.

Add 2 cups of the chicken stock along with the legs and thighs to the pot. Cover and simmer for 25 minutes.

Add 1/2 cup chicken stock, red wine and chicken breasts and simmer for 20 minutes.

CELERY SEED

Plant Family: Parsley (Umbelliferae)

Where Grown: India and Grown Worldwide

Parts Used: Seeds

Other Names: Smallage

Perhaps one of the most bitter spices, celery seed is often used in pickling, condiments, dressings and soups. Related to the celery that we are used to eating alone or using in salads, soups and stuffings, these seeds come from the Apium graveolens plant.

Celery was first used as a medicine in ancient times and then put into use as a food about 3000 years ago. It was once considered to have magical properties and was used in many ceremonies and funerals. Today it is being studied for it's reputed ability to reduce levels uric acid (which causes gout) in the body.

Seeds should be stored in an airtight container in a cool, dry and dark place. The will keep for about 6 months before they lose flavor and potency.

Health Benefits

For thousands of years numerous healthcare providers and healers have recommended celery seed to help various health issues. Celery seed is one of the least well known herbs but some individuals today use it as a diuretic. This means that certain chemicals in celery seed are able to help the body remove excess retained water in the form of urine.

In addition to this, celery seed has many other uses. As it helps to lower the amount of uric acid in the body it is often used to help treat a variety of kidney problems such as kidney stones.

Scientist have recently been studying the medical qualities of celery seed and have found evidence which suggests that the chemicals present in celery seed may be of use when treating many very common health complaints including hypertension (high blood pressure), arthritis, and anxiety. Early evidence suggests that celery seed along with celery and broccoli may help prevent cancerous cells from developing in the body.

Celery seed contains limonene, a compound which is effective as a tranquilizer, this helps to make celery seed useful as a herbal remedy to treat anxiety.

Celery seed has anti-bacterial properties, this has lead to it's use to treat urinary tract infections. These anti-bacterial ingredients also make celery seed highly suitable to treatment of the common cold and even flu.

In animals celery seed has been shown to lower blood pressure and cholesterol levels. It is also thought that celery seed can play an active role in protecting the liver particularly when taking strong pain killers which can have a negative effect on the liver. This comes as no surprise to many since one of the oldest uses for celery seed is as a liver tonic.

Celery seed may also have advantages for women as it is thought to strengthen the uterus, and help to relieve menstrual cramps by increasing the menstrual flow.

Culinary Uses

Celery is a biennial plant used in cooking for its flavor and aroma. It can be both a vegetable and a spice. The stalks, leaves and seeds can all be used in cooking. Various culinary uses of celery seed are:

The primary use of celery is soups and salads. It adds flavor while cutting down on sodium and makes a good base for vegetarian soups and sauces. In soups, the stalks and vegetables of celery are added. Add celery seeds to coleslaw recipe and potato salad recipe for that fresh and spicy taste. It adds an interesting texture along with its flavor.

Celery salt (a mixture of ground celery seeds and table salt) is used to increase the savory taste of spicy dishes.

Ground celery seeds are used in pickles for their strong flavor.

Celery seed is highly recommended in beef and meat dishes, as they increase the taste of beef. Sprinkle a quarter teaspoon of celery to one pound of beef. The ground form is used in sausages, salami, corned beef and frankfurters.

Celery is used in Old Bay seasoning (it is a dry mixture celery salt, cinnamon, ground dry mustard, cloves, ginger and paprika).

Some of the dishes in which celery is used are Chicago-style hotdog, celery seed bread and coleslaw recipe with ground celery seeds.

Celery Seed Dressing

Ingredients:

- 1/2 cup good quality wine or cider vinegar
- 1 teaspoon dry mustard
- 1 teaspoon sea salt
- 10 tablespoons sugar
- 1 cup light olive, peanut or vegetable oil
- 1 teaspoon celery seed
- Pinch of black pepper

Preparation:

Combine ingredients in large bowl and whisk together until well mixed.

Store in the refrigerator.

Zesty Chicken Salad

Ingredients:

- 2 cooked boneless, skinless chicken breast halves
- 1/4 teaspoon celery seed
- 1/4 teaspoon black pepper
- 1/4 teaspoon dijon mustard
- 1/2 cup mayonnaise
- 1/2 cup chopped celery (leaves and stalks)

Preparation:

Cut chicken into small cubes. I prefer them to be very small, almost shredded like tuna but if you prefer big chunks in your chicken salad then feel free to make them bigger.

Combine chicken with the rest of the ingredients in a large bowl.

Cover and refrigerate for 1 hour.

CHIVES

Plant Family: Onion (Liliaceae)

Where Grown: Central Europe and Central Asia

Parts Used: Leaves and Flowers

Other Names: Onion Grass

Chives with their mildly sweet onion like flavor are probably one of my favorite herbs to grow in the garden because of the beautiful purple pom-pom like flowers they produce. While the hollow tubed leaves are what is typically used, the flowers can also be eaten and have a more garlicky flavor than the leaves. Not only are they pretty to have in the garden but they also repel some insects and garden pests.

Chives are rather a delicate herb and should be used fresh. They will lose flavor quickly so it is best to use them right away. You will be able to harvest the leaves the entire growing season as the plant will continue to produce them so, keep a scissors handy and trek out to the garden to cut a handful whenever you need them.

Chives grow wild in both Europe and Asia and have been used since the 1500s in food preparation and for medicinal purposes. Medieval gardens often featured chives around the edges to help keep away insects and it is, perhaps, this use that started the practice of hanging bunches of chives in the home to ward off evil.

Chives make a great addition to most any dish, especially those that can't support the pungent flavor of onion but need a little lighter zip to them.

Health Benefits

Chives have many unsuspected health benefits for those who consume them. Like other herbs in the onion family, they have slight anti-inflammatory properties as well as antibiotic properties. These properties help in reducing the effects of rheumatoid arthritis and can be eaten to help prevent food poisoning from salmonella.

Chives also have organosulfide-containing bioflavonoids which have good anti-cancer properties, especially against stomach, colorectal and prostate cancer. However, the effect is less than that of garlic. These bioflavonoids also help to lower blood pressure.

Chives also have anti fungal properties and can help reduce flatulence and bad breath as well as prevent colds. They can also have a diuretic affect.

Chives are rich in folic acid, vitamins A, C, E and K, iron, calcium, zinc and also include traces of other vitamins and minerals.

Because many of the beneficial compounds are destroyed by heat, chives are best consumed raw. As such, they are less pungent than raw onions or garlic so more benefit might be obtained from them than you might think by doing a simple comparison between the three.

Chives are safe for most people in food amounts as well as medicinal amounts. Taking too much (medicinally) may cause upset stomach.

Culinary Uses

Chives are a great tasting herb that can add a extra dimension to a simple dish. Their mild onion taste makes them excellent as an simple yet effective way of enhancing a smooth cream cheese.

Fresh chives are utilized in French cooking in this way. A simple starter dish is a good quality Brie cheese served with chopped fresh chives and fresh smoked salmon served on a sliced, lightly toasted baguette. These good quality flavorful ingredients will combine to produce a delicious starter which is very easy to make and very impressive.

Chives are also widely used in England during cooking. Often combined with cheese like the French but also used in many other dishes such as creamed potatoes with butter to add a subtle but interesting taste. They are often used in this way to add interest to a bland food. Many cultures also value chives as a garnish to add color and a professional touch to a finished dish.

Chives are used in most countries and can be a great addition to any dish.

Sour Cream And Chive Garlic Mashed Potatoes

Ingredients:

- 2 pounds boiling potatoes cut into large cubes
- 6 cloves garlic peeled
- 1/2 cup milk
- 1/2 cup sour cream
- 1/4 cup chives
- 1/2 teaspoon salt
- 1/8 teaspoon pepper

Preparation:

Add potatoes and garlic to a large pot and fill with water to cover the potatoes.

Bring to a boil and cook until potatoes are tender when pierced with a fork (about 20 minutes).

Drain and put in large bowl.

Mash potatoes adding in the milk, sour cream and chives. Either hand mash or mash with an electric beater.

Add salt and pepper to taste.

Buttermilk Chive Dressing

Ingredients:

- 1/4 cup fresh chives
- 1/4 teaspoon salt
- 1/4 teaspoon pepper
- 1 teaspoon sugar
- 1/4 - 1/2 cup buttermilk
- 2/3 cup mayonnaise

Preparation:

Mix all the ingredients together adding more or less buttermilk depending on how thick you want it to be. Refrigerate for at least an hour before use.

CILANTRO

Plant Family: Parsley (Umbelliferae)

Where Grown: Southern Europe, North Africa, Southwestern Asia

Parts Used: Leaves, roots, seeds and stem

Other Names: Coriander leaf, Chinese parsley

Cilantro is an integral part of Latin and Asian cooking and has an unmistakable lemony mustard flavor with an herbal tang. Popular in curries, this herb is great in both cold and cooked dishes. The leaves are what is predominantly used in cooking but the seeds can also be used although they have a stronger, spicier taste. The roots are used in Thai cooking and have a stronger flavor than the leaves.

The use of cilantro can be traced back to 5,000 BC. It was cultivated in ancient Egypt, used by both ancient Greek and Roman cultures and even mentioned in the bible. Hippocrates used it as a medicinal herb and cilantro seeds were found in King Tuts tomb. It is thought to have aphrodisiac properties and the Chinese used it in love potions.

Cilantro has one strange characteristic and that is that some people cannot stand it as it tastes like soap to them. This is particularly true when the herb is raw and cooking may make it more palatable for these people.

Health Benefits

It's not surprising that cilantro has been a valued herb among healers for centuries. Cilantro is not only mentioned in ancient texts across many cultures, but its seeds and stems have been found in Egyptian tombs. Modern scientific studies of cilantro prove that ancient medical practitioners knew what they were doing in selecting cilantro as an agent for healing.

Cilantro leaves are rich in an array of something called anti-oxidant polyphenolic flavonoids, including quercetin, kaempferol, rhamnetin and epigenin. Flavonoids are now well understood to provide protection against allergens. They also serve as anti-inflammatory agents and almost certainly lower the human body's chance of developing cancer. Flavonoids are sometimes called Vitamin P and cilantro is rich in this substance.

Another major health benefit of cilantro is that it can help lower LDL or "bad" cholesterol, while also raising HDL or "good" cholesterol.

Furthermore, eating cilantro is almost like taking a multi-vitamin. Here is an amazing list of the vitamins found in cilantro: Vitamin C, folic acid, Vitamin K, riboflavin, niacin, and Vitamin A, not to mention beta-carotene. In fact, 100 grams of cilantro would provide 225% of the human body's daily need for Vitamin A.

The human body also needs trace elements of basic minerals and metals to stay healthy, such as iron, manganese, calcium, potassium - and cilantro has all of them.

When cilantro is dried and ground into a spice it is called coriander. Coriander seeds, which are essentially the seeds of the cilantro plant, are frequently used as an analgesic. The seeds are also employed as an anti-spasmodic agent, digestive aide, carminative (prevents gas) an anti-fungal agent. Coriander seeds are sometimes even used as a weight-loss stimulant.

Cilantro is well known as a detoxifying herb that can leech metals from the body. It also has antibacterial properties and can help kill of viruses that cause colds. Cilantro is also known to contain anti-inflammatory properties that minimizes rheumatoid arthritis, prevent Chron's disease, and many other immune disorders. It also contains a large amount of Borneol, an organic alcohol produced naturally by cilantro, capable of destroying viruses and germs that causes colds and flu. It is also known to increase production of gastric juices in the stomach which help the digestive system.

Cilantro is safe in food amounts as well as when taken medicinally in appropriate doses. It may cause increased sensitivity to the sun and allergic reactions.

Culinary Uses

Cilantro is used in many dishes around the world including Mediterranean, Indian, American, Asian, Mexican and African foods. I can be added to salsas and other dips, curries, used in chutneys and relishes, put into marinades, and used to flavor soups, stews and vegetable stir fries (such as Thai or Chinese). You can additionally use it as a garnish or in salads.

When using this herb you need to chop it up and then add it near the end of cooking so that it doesn't shrivel up or get too soggy. The flavor is also reduced by intense cooking. Ideally it should be used raw to add a stronger flavor to the food.

My favorite uses of this herb are in a salad with ginger and carrots, or in lentil soup. It also adds a lovely flavor to Indian foods and works well in a salad served with Indian starters or sprinkled over warm naan bread.

Make sure that you use this herb fresh as most of the flavor is lost in the drying process. If you want to store it for a while, it is much better to freeze it and take it out of the freezer as needed. The best way to use it, however, is to grow your own plant so you can harvest it when you need it. This will give you the best flavor and freshness.

Cilantro Chicken

Ingredients:

- 2 Pounds boneless, skinless chicken breasts
- 1/2 cup fresh cilantro, chopped
- 6 cloves garlic, chopped
- 1/4 cup lime juice
- 1/4 cup olive oil
- 1 tablespoon honey
- 1/2 teaspoon salt
- 1/2 teaspoon pepper

Preparation:

Put the chicken breast in a shallow dish.

Whisk the rest of the ingredients together in a bowl and pour over the chicken.

Cover and marinate for at least 1 hour.

Grill chicken in grill pan or on barbecue grill.

Cashew Cilantro Couscous

Ingredients:

- 3 cups couscous
- 3 cups water
- 1/2 cup olive oil
- 3/4 cup fresh cilantro, chopped
- 1/4 cup fresh mint, chopped
- 1 cup cashews, chopped

Preparation:

Bring water to a boil in small pan.

Remove water from heat and add couscous. Cover and let stand until the couscous has absorbed the water.

Stir in the rest of the ingredients.

CINNAMON

Plant Family: Laurel (Lauraceae)

Where Grown: Sri Lanka

Parts Used: Inner bark

Other Names: Baker's cinnamon, soft stick cinnamon

Probably one of the most well known spices, cinnamon evokes the warm feelings of holidays and home. It's used extensively in baking and is one of the "warm" spices that can help with a host of health problems.

Most people don't realize that cinnamon is the inner bark of a tree that is native to South East Asia and comes in rolled up tubes, kind of like a scroll. The tube is then grated to produce the powder we use in baking or the whole thing can be used in savory dishes or drinks.

Today, cinnamon is commonly found in almost every kitchen, but it was once very rare and highly sought after. In fact, the quest for cinnamon was one of the things that fueled the exploration of the new world.

Cinnamon is an ancient spice which was used in Egypt since 2000 BCE and recorded in the Bible. One of it's primary uses was to mask the taste and smell of spoiled meat. Coincidentally, cinnamon contains phenols that inhibit the growth of bacteria so it turns out it was a great choice for the task.

Health Benefits

Cinnamon has a lot of health benefits and is a traditional warming spice used to help treat the cold or flu. It also has anti-fungal, anti-inflammatory and anti-bacterial properties and can help control blood sugar as well as cholesterol levels.

Cinnamon can also decrease the pain that may be experienced by people suffering from arthritis - it greatly reduces the pain associated with the joints and encourages mobility.

An interesting study showed that smelling cinnamon can help give the brain the boost that is needed to perform better. Smelling it may help your mental performance and memory.

Due to the anti-fungal and anti-bacterial properties, it is thought that cinnamon may also help in clearing infections from the body.

Culinary Uses

Cinnamon is one of the favorite kitchen spices in the world today. It can be found in almost every country and in some cultures is considered to be an essential spice which has a wide variety of culinary uses. From tea to bread, this spice can be found in many different dishes and many styles of cooking.

Cinnamon is most popular among bakers, as it adds a special kick to almost any pie or cookie. Cinnamon is a versatile spice which can also be found far outside the world of baking. It is commonly used in dishes with squash, sauces or rubs for meats, even pasta and chili.

Other common applications of cinnamon include spiced beverages such as cocoa or coffee and spice mixes used in different cultures to create unique flavors and dishes.

Some culinary experts believe that any dish can be improved with cinnamon, provided it is used in the proper way.

Cinnamon Maple Squash

Ingredients:

- 7 cups butternut squash, cubed
- 3 tablespoons butter, melted
- 1/4 cup maple syrup
- 1/2 teaspoon ground cinnamon
- 1/2 tablespoon brown sugar
- 1/4 teaspoon salt

Preparation:

Preheat oven to 400F.

Put squash in a big bowl and toss with butter and maple syrup.

Combine cinnamon, brown sugar and salt and mix in with squash mixture, coating the squash evenly.

Lay squash out in a shallow baking dish or cookie sheet.

Bake for 40 minutes.

Cinnamon Cookies

Ingredients:

- 1 cup salted butter
- 3/4 cup brown sugar, packed
- 3/4 cup white sugar
- 2 eggs
- 2 teaspoons vanilla extract
- 1 teaspoon cinnamon
- 1/4 teaspoon salt
- 2 1/2 cups flour
- 1/2 teaspoon baking soda

Topping:

Mix 1 tablespoon cinnamon with 3 tablespoons white sugar in a shallow bowl.

Preparation:

Preheat oven to 300F.

Combine flour, salt and soda in a medium bowl. Whisk together well.

Mix the brown and white sugars together in a large bowl. Add butter and mix well. Add eggs and vanilla. Mix until fluffy.

Add flour mixture to the egg and sugar mixture and blend until just mixed. Do not over mix.

Make 1" balls with the dough. Dip each ball in the topping mixture and roll around to cover the whole ball.

Bake or 18 minutes on an un-greased cookie sheet. Place balls 2" apart.

FENNEL

Plant Family: Parsley (Umbelliferae)
Where Grown: Indigenous to the Mediterranean and now cultivated in Most Countries In The Northern Hemisphere

Parts Used: Seeds, Leaves, Roots

Other Names: Sweet Fennel Florence Fennel

Fennel has been used in northern Mediterranean cultures since the times of the ancient Romans were it was a symbol of good health and prosperity. It was also popular in India and China. Charlemagne declared it an essential herb as far back as 812 and it was often chewed during church in medieval times to stop gastric rumblings. Church was probably an appropriate place for it because it was also used to ward off ghosts and protect against evil.

In modern times, perhaps the most recognized use for this spice is in Italian sausage where the seeds are known for their licorice taste.

Fennel grows in many countries these days and can even be found growing wild by the side of the road. It is an aromatic perennial that can grow to be 5 feet tall and has tiny yellow flowers.

Health Benefits

Fennel is a cleansing herb and often associated with digestive healing. Fennel teas made from the seeds and oils of the plant have been used since ancient times to treat a variety of problems including kidney stones, gout, jaundice, nausea and even hiccups. This herb is believed to be an appetite suppressant and, therefore has been used to promote weight loss. It has long been used to aid in digestion and is reputed to help the system digest fat.

Like many herbs, fennel can be used for a variety of medicinal purposes but it is mainly used as a carminative, diuretic and mild stimulant. It is also thought to help detoxify the liver, help clear urinary tract problems and even treat colic in babies. Hippocrates said this herb could help stimulate milk production for nursing mothers.

Today, fennel may have its medicinal uses as well, in fact it has shown to help detoxify the liver and preliminary studies show that regularly eating fennel may help slow down osteoporosis. A study done in 2003 at Ataturk University suggest that the antioxidant properties of fennel are quite effective in fighting free radicals.

For healing uses, mostly the seeds and oils are used other than for urinary tract disorders in which the roots are used. As with any essential oil, care should be taken with use and infants and people with epilepsy should avoid using the oils of fennel.

Culinary Uses

Fennel bulbs, leafs and seeds can be used in cooking but it is the seed that we are most familiar with and which flavors Italian sausage. The seeds also go particularly well with fish, can also be used with any meat dish and are often found in baked breads and desserts.

When using the bulb in cooking, you want to look for Florence fennel but for the seeds and leaves you want sweet fennel.

Fennel bulbs should be white and firm. You can cut them up and they can be served on their own marinated, roasted, grilled or braised. The stocks can also be used and can sometimes be found in salads or used as an interesting substitute for celery. The leaves have a licorice taste and can be used as a garnish or put into soups, stews or salads.

Braised Fennel

Ingredients:

- 2 fennel bulbs with fronds
- 1 1/2 tablespoons extra-virgin olive oil
- 1 teaspoon salt
- 1 teaspoon sugar
- 1/2 cup reduced-sodium chicken broth
- 1/2 cup water

Preparation:

Cut the tops from the Fennel bulbs. Cut each bulb in half and then into quarters - leave the core attached on each piece so they don't fall apart.

Chop the fennel fronds.

Heat the oil in a skillet over medium-high heat

Place the fennel bulbs into the skillet and reduce heat to medium

Brown the slices for about 2 minutes then turn over and brown the other side.

Sprinkle the salt and sugar over the fennel

Reduce the heat to low and add the broth and water

Cook covered on low until the fennel is tender - about 15 minutes.

Sprinkle the chopped fennel fronds over the dish before serving.

Fennel Cookies

Ingredients:

- 3 cups flour
- 1 teaspoon baking powder
- 1/2 teaspoon salt
- 1 cup sugar
- 1 cup butter, unsalted, softened
- 2 eggs
- 2 1/2 tablespoon fennel seeds, crushed
- 1 tablespoon vanilla extract
- 3 tablespoons turbinado sugar

Preparation:

Sift flour, baking powder and salt together in a small bowl.

In a large bowl, beat butter until creamy, gradually add the sugar and beat until light and fluffy.

Add eggs, one at a time to the butter mixture beating well after each addition.

Add the flour, salt and baking soda mixture to the butter mixture and stir until blended.

Add the fennel seeds and vanilla.

Roll dough into 2 12" long logs.

Freeze dough for at least 2 hours.

When dough is firm, preheat over to 350F .

Cut dough into 1/4 inch slices.

Sprinkle slices with sugar.

Bake on un-greased cookie sheets for 10 minutes.

FENUGREEK

Plant Family: Bean (Fabaceae)

Where Grown: Indigenous to the Eastern Mediterranean and now grown in India, Turkey, Egypt, Morocco, China and France

Parts Used: Seeds and Leaves

Other Names: Goat's Horn, Greek Hayseed, Birds Foot

Fenugreek is one of the oldest cultivated plants and was a favorite of Hippocrates and also used by Dioscorides. The Egyptians used it to embalm their dead and the ancient Romans used it as a cover crop and feed for livestock. Today you will find it favored in curries, soups and stews.

This annual herb grows to about 3 feet in height and has light green leaves and white flowers. It produces seed pods that have about 10 to 20 hard flat seeds in them. The seeds are so hard, that practical use dictates that you grind them with a mortar and pestle. This herb has a nutty taste which can be on the sweet side when cooked but can easily turn bitter.

The seeds themselves are usually ground for use in cooking, but the oils extracted from the seeds are used commercially in a lot of flavorings including vanilla, caramel butterscotch and maple.

These seeds impart a butterscotch-like smell but they actually taste more bitter than they smell. To use them properly, you want to dry them, then grind them and then cook them but you'll need to do this right before you use it in the dish because they will quickly turn bitter.

Health Benefits

The main health benefits of fenugreek stem from the fact that it contains a compound called diosgenin which has properties similar to estrogen. Because of this, it's been used to treat a myriad of menopausal and reproduction problems , including increasing libido, lessening the severity of hot flashes, increasing male potency and lessening the symptoms of PMS and menopause. It is even said to help induce childbirth by stimulating uterine contractions (pregnant woman should consult their doctor before using fenugreek for this purpose).

Fenugreek also has been traditionally used to treat a host of other problems not the least of which is normalizing your cholesterol and blood sugar levels. In fact, studies have shown that people with type II diabetes had lower blood sugar levels after eating 500 mg of fenugreek daily.

This herb is also a natural remedy for heartburn and acid reflux because the seeds contain a lot of mucilage which coats the lining of the stomach and helps soothe inflammation.

In addition to diosgenin, fenugreek seeds also contain vitamin C, niacin, potassium and protein.

This herb is generally considered a safe herb especially when taken in food amounts but could cause nausea or digestive upset if too much is taken. It is not recommended to use this during pregnancy. Fenugreek fiber can interfere with absorption of other medicines so you want to be sure to wait several hours after eating fenugreek before you take any medications.

Culinary Uses

Fenugreek is often found used in curries, but it can also complement meats poultry and vegetables. You must use it in moderation because too much of it will cause your food to taste bitter. It is also to be noted that the raw seeds are more bitter so you should always use them dried and ground because the seeds are too hard to eat whole.

Fenugreek leaves have a peanut-like taste and are used either fresh or dried. They go particularly well with spinach, potatoes and carrots.

In Egypt and Ethiopia you will find fenugreek being used in a lot of breads.

A popular use of the seeds today is to sprout them and add them to salads and vegetable dishes.

Curry Powder

Ingredients:

- 2 teaspoons fenugreek seed
- 2 teaspoons coriander (ground)
- 2 teaspoons turmeric
- 1 1/2 teaspoon cumin seeds
- 1/2 teaspoon black peppercorns
- 1/2 teaspoon crushed red pepper flakes
- 1 teaspoon ground cinnamon
- 1/4 teaspoon ground ginger
- 1/2 oz mustard seed

Preparation:

Put everything in a blender or food processor and cover

Grind until the mixture turns to a fine powder - about 2 minutes.

Store in an airtight glass container in a cool dry place.

Fenugreek Chicken

Ingredients:

- 2 pounds chicken breast cubed
- 1 cup fenugreek leaves
- 2 onions
- 3/4 teaspoon ginger garlic paste
- 1 teaspoon green chili paste
- 1/2 teaspoon cumin
- 1 tomato, pureed
- 1/4 cup yogurt
- 1/8 teaspoon turmeric
- 3/4 teaspoon red chili powder
- 2 tablespoons coconut oil

Preparation:

Sauté the onions and a little bit of oil until browned then run them through a food processor until they are like a paste.

Sauté the fenugreek leaves in 2 teaspoons of oil until they crisp - about 8 minutes.

Remove from pan and set aside.

In the same pan, heat the rest of the oil and add ginger garlic paste and green chili paste and sauté for 4 minutes.

Add turmeric, red chili powder and cumin to the pan and stir.

Add tomato puree, cook for 3 minutes.

Add onion paste, cook for 3 minutes.

Add chicken, stir and cook on medium-high for 4 minutes while stirring.

Reduce to medium, cover the pot and cook until the chicken is almost done.

Add the fenugreek leaves and continue cooking until chicken is done.

GARLIC

Plant Family: Onion (Alliaceae)

Where Grown: Originating in central Asia, China is the largest producer of garlic followed by India and then South Korea but it can be grown in any mild climate.

Parts Used: Bulbs and Leaves

Garlic is perhaps one of the most recognized herbs and flavors dishes in almost every cuisine from Italian to Asian. It is an ancient plant and has been used since Neolithic times. Not only is garlic great for flavoring food, but it also has very powerful medicinal properties.

Although it has been used for its healing properties since ancient times, many cultures did not find it suitable for food use until later on. In Victorian times it was considered too pungent and in the famous Victorian cookbook by Mrs Beeton it was said "the smell of this plant is generally considered offensive and it is the most acrimonious in its taste".

The Buddhists and highborn Hindus did not use it in food and it was forbidden by monks who thought it could arouse passions. In addition to that, anyone who had taken a chastity vow, widows and adolescents were forbidden from eating it because of its stimulating qualities.

Garlic has a long history in Ayurvedic medicine as it is said to possess 5 of the 6 tastes defined in the system. It was also thought that hanging garlic on your door could help stop the spread of smallpox, and we all know that a garlic clove necklace can do wonders to ward off vampires.

Aristotle mentions the value of garlic and Pliny the Elder prescribes it in his "Historia Naturalis". Indeed, the use of garlic for medicinal purposes can be found to have roots in many cultures around the world. In 1858, the antibacterial properties of garlic were recorded by Louis Pasteur and it was even used in World War I and World War II to help control infections in wounds.

Today, we recognize its pungent taste in many foods. It is related to onions, leeks and chives and is a root crop. The bulb which grows underground is harvested in July or August and this is the part that you eat. Garlic is a forgiving plant and can be grown in poor soils and harsh climates.

Health Benefits

Garlic is perhaps one of the most popular of the healing herbs. It has antibacterial and anti-fungal properties and can be used to heal many ills. The active ingredient in garlic, allicin, is strongest about 5 - 10 minutes after you chop up the clove and loses its potency when you cook it so in order to get the most healing benefits from garlic, you will want to crush the cloves and then eat them raw about 5 or 10 min. later.

Garlic is said to help with a host of blood related problems. It has been shown to help reduce cholesterol and control blood pressure as well as thin the blood which can help prevent clotting. It can also help to dilate your blood vessels.

One of the interesting applications of garlic for healing is to help prevent the common cold. In fact, a study of 150 people showed that those who took garlic supplements daily had fewer incidents of colds than those who took a placebo.

I actually use garlic myself when I feel the very beginnings of a cold coming on. I crush the garlic bulb and spread it on toast. That combined with some extra vitamin C seems to ward off the cold more times than not as long as I catch it very early.

Garlic also has anti-fungal properties and topical creams with garlic may help fight infections. One small study showed that a garlic cream applied topically helped to resolve athlete's foot.

Garlic is also a powerful antioxidant and has Vitamin C, B6, selenium, potassium, magnesium, calcium, manganese and flavonoids.

One thing to note is that raw garlic can be very strong and irritating to your mouth and digestive tract so you want to be really careful when eating it raw. Some people are allergic to garlic and if you get rashes or headaches after eating garlic you might consider that you have an allergy.

Culinary Uses

Garlic is used to flavor almost anything from meats to soups and most people feel every dish is much better with it included. It can be used whole, minced, crushed or chopped to any degree. The finer you chop it and the darker you let it get while cooking the sharper the taste will be. One word of caution, even if you love the taste of garlic it can quickly overpower the other ingredients in your dish so you want to use it judiciously.

Be very careful not to burn your garlic as this will turn it bitter and ruin it for food use. Also take care to remove any green sprouts from the center as this will cause the garlic to be bitter as well.

For cooking purposes, the giant heads called elephant garlic may seem appealing because of their size but they're actually not as suitable as the regular smaller heads of garlic so you always want to go for the regular garlic when shopping. In addition to that, buying the pre-minced garlic may be convenient but it will not taste as good as garlic that you mince yourself from a fresh bulb.

Garlic can be eaten raw or cooked but the raw garlic is very pungent and can be irritating to the pallet. Cooked garlic will become sweeter and milder but, as mentioned above, you need to be careful not to burn it as this will turn it bitter and ruin your dish. Cooking it slowly at a lower temperature is the preferred method.

If you love to eat garlic but are worried about having garlic breath, it is reputed that chewing fresh parsley can help remedy this. Interestingly enough, many dishes that use garlic also include parsley.

Roasted Garlic Soup

Ingredients:

- 4 garlic bulbs
- 1/4 cup olive oil
- 6 tablespoons butter
- 1 onion, chopped
- 4 leeks, chopped
- 6 tablespoons flour
- 4 cups chicken broth
- 1 cup heavy cream
- Pinch salt
- Pepper to taste
- Handful of chopped chives

Preparation:

Cut off the tops of each garlic head so that the very top of each bulb is cut off (cut about 1/4" from the top).

Put garlic heads in a shallow baking dish, cut site up and drizzle the olive oil over them.

Bake at 350F for 1 hour until garlic is golden. Remove and cool.

After they are cool, remove the bulbs and chop.

Heat butter in a large saucepan on medium until melted.

Add garlic, onion and leeks to pan and sauté until onion is translucent.

Add flour and cook for 10 minutes, stirring it until it turns into a rue.

Add chicken broth, cover and simmer for 20 minutes.

Cool the soup a bit and then transfer to a blender of food processor and puree.

Return the pureed soup to the saucepan and add the cream, simmer about 10 minutes until it thickens.

Add salt and pepper to taste.

Pour in bowls, add chives to the top as a garnish and enjoy!

Garlic Mashed Potatoes

Ingredients:

- 3 1/2 pounds russet potatoes
- 2 tablespoons salt
- 1 cup cream
- 1 cup 1% milk
- 2 tablespoons butter
- 6 cloves garlic, crushed

Preparation:

Peel potatoes and cut into 1" cubes.

Put potatoes in a large pot of water and add salt.

Bring water to a boil, then reduce to maintain the boil without boiling over.

Put the milk, cream and garlic into a small saucepan and heat on medium until it simmers then remove from the heat.

Cook the potatoes until they fall apart when poked.

Drain the water and transfer potatoes to a large bowl.

Add the cream and garlic mixture and the butter to the potatoes and whip or mash until you get the desired consistency. You can add more milk if they are too dry. Also, it might be smart to add the cream mixture in increments to avoid having your potatoes get too liquidy.

GINGER

Plant Family: Ginger (Zingiberaceae)

Where Grown: China, Australis, India and many tropical regions.

Parts Used: Root

Other Names: Ginger Root

Ginger is perhaps one of the most pungent spices with its combination of sweet, zesty and hot flavors. It is a very versatile spice and can be used in almost every type of meal from appetizer to desert. Its history goes back over 5000 years and it is traditionally considered a general tonic for what ails you.

Originating in Southeast Asia, ginger has long been cultivated in other countries. The Romans used it very early on but it almost disappeared from that culture when the Roman Empire fell. Thankfully, Marco Polo returned from China with a fresh batch and its use came into favor once again even though it was quite costly to buy.

Ginger is considered a warming spice coming from the same family as turmeric and cardamom and has been used in Eastern medicine for thousands of years. Although initially used as a healing spice, it eventually became popular to use in cooking and even more so when Queen Elizabeth I of England used it to create the first ginger bread man.

The part of the plant that is used for both cooking and healing is the rhizome, or root of the plant. The plant itself grows well in tropical climates and is popular throughout the Caribbean. It is a perennial plant with a reedy look that grows to about 3 or 4 feet tall and produces white and pink flower buds which bloom into yellow flowers. The ginger root itself is harvested when the stock withers at the end of the growing season.

Health Benefits

Ginger has long been used to prevent nausea and, in fact, we still use it for this in the form of ginger ale that we often drink when we are feeling sick. This isn't just an old wives tale though, as many modern studies have found that ginger is more effective than a placebo for seasickness, morning sickness and nausea due to chemotherapy.

Ginger is an excellent carminative, which means that it effectively eliminates intestinal gas and it is also an anti-spasmodic so it has long been used for intestinal problems.

It also has anti-inflammatory compounds which have been shown to help arthritis sufferers manage their pain. In two clinical studies involving the use of ginger to control pain it was found that 75% of arthritis patients and 100% of patients with muscle pain experienced relief when taking ginger.

Ginger may also be effective in fighting cancer. Research presented at a major meeting of cancer experts (Frontiers in Cancer Prevention Research) showed that it may inhibit the growth of human colorectal cancer cells based on research done with mice at Minnesota's Hormel Institute. Another study done by Dr. Rebecca Lui at the University of Michigan showed that the active nutrients and ginger can cause ovarian cancer cells to self-destruct.

This warming herb can also help stimulate circulation and has natural blood thinning properties. It is said to be able to help relieve symptoms of the common cold because it can stimulate the secretion of mucus and soothe your store throat as well as boost your immune system to help your body battle illness. In addition to that, it's powerful anti-viral, anti-inflammatory and anti-fungal properties help fight the virus that causes the common cold.

The enzymes in ginger can help aid in digestion and prevent cramping so it is a perfect herb to add to most any dish. In fact, the agent Greeks used to eat ginger after a meal in order to help the digestive process along.

Culinary Uses

Ginger can be consumed in a variety of ways - fresh, dried, ground, crystallized and even pickled. No only that, but it can be used in a variety of meals from appetizers to salads to dinners to desserts making it one of the most versatile herbs available.

For culinary use, ginger is most often used either powdered or fresh. If you are buying fresh ginger, you want to be aware that the younger rhizomes are milder in taste so depending on your purpose you may want to pick a younger root or if you want a more pungent taste choose an older one. The younger the root is, the thinner the papery skin will be.

Ginger is often used as a marinade as well as in curries and stir fries. In the Western world it is more popular in baking and candy making.

Ginger can be sliced, diced, chopped, pureed, grated or minced depending on your needs. The ginger itself can be a bit tough to chew so if you don't want that element in your food then it's best to grate it, that being said, if you are roasting or stir frying the ginger small slivers can add an interesting element to the dish.

Grated Carrots with Ginger

Ingredients:

• 2 teaspoons coconut oil (substitute canola oil if you don't have coconut oil handy)
• 3 cups grated carrots
• 1 teaspoons minced ginger
• 1/2 cup orange juice (fresh is best!)
• Salt and pepper to taste

Preparation:

Heat oil in a skillet over medium heat.

Add carrots and ginger and cook for 2 minutes.

Stir in orange juice and pinch of salt.

Simmer uncovered until carrots are tender and most of the liquid has evaporated - this will take about 5 or 10 minutes.

Season with pepper to taste.

Healthy Ginger Cookies

Ingredients:

- 1/4 cup molasses
- 1 cup brown sugar
- 3/4 cup canola oil
- 1 egg
- 2 1/4 cups whole wheat flour
- 1/4 teaspoon salt
- 2 teaspoons baking soda
- 1 teaspoon cinnamon
- 1 1/2 teaspoons powdered ginger

Preparation:

Preheat oven to 350F

In a large bowl, combine brown sugar, molasses, egg and oil.

Whisk together the rest of the ingredients in a small bowl.

Stir the dry ingredients into the wet ingredients.

Drop by rounded tablespoon onto un-greased cookie sheets

Bake for about 8 minutes at 350F.

HORSERADISH

Plant Family: Cruciferae

Where Grown: Asia, Russia, Most Countries In Northern Hemisphere

Parts Used: Roots and Leaves

Other Names: Horse Root, Mountain Radish

Horseradish with its pungent, spicy, mustard-like flavor is perhaps best known for its pairing with roast beef and has been used since ancient times as both a medicinal and culinary herb.

The Egyptians and early Greeks used both the leaves and roots for their medicinal properties and the plant is even depicted in a mural found in the ancient city of Pompeii. The first culinary record of this herb dates to John Gerard's book "*Herball*" in 1597, but there are many mentions of it as a medicinal herb before that.

Horseradish is one of the few plants that is actually still harvested by hand and can be grown in most northern climates. The roots are what are typically used and those are harvested just before winter after the leaves have died off of the plant.

The horseradish plant itself makes a good addition to any herb garden and it is quite hardy and easy to grow. It has its tall wide, crinkly leaves that can grow to be 2 feet in height. It grows as a perennial in zones 2-9 and as an annual in other zones. This herb can be very invasive as it produces other plants from its shoots. In fact, these young shoots are what should be dug up as they are the tastiest part of the plant. Horseradish grows from root cuttings and can be grown in the garden or in a deep, wide pot.

Health Benefits

You've probably experienced the sinus clearing effects of eating hot, spicy foods and for this, horseradish is the best of the best. In fact, it can be quite effective in treating sinus problems when eaten as well as applied in a poultice to the forehead. It also has antibiotic properties that can be used to fight bacteria in the throat which causes bronchitis and coughing.

These antibiotic properties combined with the fact that is also a diuretic can help fight urinary tract infections. It is been shown to be so powerful that the German commission E has approved it as an additional treatment to be used with prescription drugs for UTI's.

Since horseradish stimulates blood flow to the surface of the skin it can help relieve muscle aches and pains and has been seen to be effective in treating rheumatism when applied in a poultice topically to the skin.

Like many herbs, horseradish can aid in digestion because it is a gastric stimulant which helps the salivary and intestinal glands to produce digestive enzymes. It is also an anti-inflammatory herb as well as a diuretic and can have a soothing effect on your nerves.

Horseradish contains glucosinolates which can help your liver detoxify carcinogens from the body and may also help suppress the growth of tumors. Two separate studies, one at the University of Illinois and one at the University of Dundee in Scotland, indicate that eating large amounts of glucosinolates can help boost humans' resistance to cancer.

In addition to that, the Cornell University Department of animal science says that plants containing glucosinolates may help to protect against rectal and colon cancer.

Horseradish is low in fat and calories and contains a good amount of vitamin C as well as folate, vitamin B6, riboflavin, niacin, potassium, iron, manganese, copper, zinc, magnesium and also dietary fiber.

One thing to keep in mind if you're using horseradish topically is that it can be irritating to the skin. Individuals with renal illness, gastric ulcer or goitrous problems as well as children under the age of 4 should not consume horseradish.

Culinary Uses

For cooking, the grated root of the plant is what is most often used. It is best to use this fresh as it can turn bitter as it ages. The white, tender parts of the root are what is the most tasty and the younger roots are the best.

Sometimes you'll hear the term "prepared horseradish" and that refers to the root mixed with vinegar. This will preserve the taste of the root and can be kept in the refrigerator for several months. Most recipes actually use prepared horseradish including the two I have below.

Horseradish sauce is probably the most popular use of this herb and that is the prepared horseradish mixed with cream or mayonnaise. You often find it served with roast beef. You might also find horseradish in cocktail sauce and bloody Mary's.

You can buy horseradish root in the vegetable section of your grocery store and grate it as you need it. Be aware that the fumes can be very pungent to the lungs and eyes so take care not to inhale it or get any of the juice in your eyes.

Grated horseradish can add a wonderful dimension to dips, soups, sauces, sandwiches and side dishes.

Prepared Horseradish

Ingredients:

- 10" horseradish root
- 2 Tablespoons water
- 1 Tablespoon white vinegar
- Pinch Salt

Preparation:

Peel the outer coating from the root so that the inner white part is exposed.

Cut the root up and place in food processor along with the water.

Process until it is almost like a paste (Be very careful as this concoction is highly irritating to lungs and eyes).

Drain out any excess water.

Add vinegar and salt to the foot processor and pulse until combined. Note that adding the vinegar stops the enzymatic process that makes the horseradish "hot" so if you want hotter prepared horseradish then wait up to 3 minutes before adding the vinegar, if you want it more mild then add the vinegar right away.

Store in glass jar, refrigerated for up to 4 weeks.

Horseradish Dill Sauce

Ingredients:

- 3 tablespoons prepared horseradish
- 1/4 cup sour cream
- 1 tablespoon mayonnaise
- 1 teaspoon dijon mustard
- 1 tablespoon chopped dill

Preparation

Mix all ingredients together and enjoy with beef, fish or pork!

Horseradish Cheese & Dill Omelet

Ingredients:

- 2 Eggs
- 1 Tablespoon milk
- 1 1/2 teaspoons prepared horseradish
- 1/2 cup grated cheddar cheese
- 1/2 tablespoon chopped dill
- Salt and pepper to taste

Preparation:

Whisk the eggs together with the milk slightly.

Pour egg mixture into skillet warmed up on medium heat.

Cook until almost done then flip over.

Add cheese and horseradish and dill evenly to the top of the omelet.

Sprinkle on salt and pepper to taste.

Cook until egg is cooked through, fold omelet in half and serve!

LEMON BALM

Plant Family: Mint (Lamiaceae)

Where Grown: Southern Parts Of Europe and South America

Parts Used: Whole Plant

Other Names: Balm Mint, Blue Balm, Honey Plant, Sweet Balm, Sweet Melissa

Lemon Balm, a member of the mint family, dates back to before the Middle Ages when it was used in wine to lift the spirits, as an herbal remedy for insect bites and as a treatment for healing wounds.

The herb is native to Europe but is now grown all over the world and grows wild in many places. Its lemony aromatic scent attracts bees to your garden and makes it a favorite herb for use in cosmetics, furniture polish and even some medicines.

Lemon balm can be grown in zones 4-9. It grows in clumps with each plant reaching about 2-3 feet in height and sporting small white flowers in the summer. You can easily propagate this herb by taking cuttings of the stem and rooting them in water then planting them after the roots have sprouted.

Health Benefits

Lemon balm is a very calming herb and can be helpful in treating insomnia and anxiety. Several studies have shown that lemon balm combined with other calming herbs like chamomile and valerian can help promote sleep and reduce anxious feelings.

This herb has also shown to improve mental performance as well as mood and there have even been positive results in small clinical trials involving Alzheimer's patients with mild and moderate symptoms.

 As a topical ointment, lemon balm may be effective in healing cold sores and might even help reduce the severity of herpes outbreaks. This is probably due to its antibacterial and antiviral properties. The leaves themselves when crushed and rubbed on your skin can act as a natural mosquito repellent and it can also be used to treat insect bites, bug stings and cuts and scrapes.

Traditionally, lemon balm tea was thought to be an anti-aging concoction and there are many stories of individuals who lived to very advanced ages due to drinking a lemon balm tea everyday. Whether or not this is true is not for me to say, however lemon balm does have many health benefits so drinking some of it each day surely can't hurt.

Recent research has found that lemon balm can help reduce oxidative stress. A study on radiology staff who were exposed to low-dose radiation due to their work found that taking lemon balm tea resulted in a significant improvement in plasma levels of catalase after 30 days.

Lemon balm is also good for relieving digestive problems and can help reduce fever due to its ability to increase sweating.

Lemon balm essential oil is very popular in aromatherapy for treating insomnia, nervousness and headaches.

Culinary Uses

As the name implies, lemon balm has a lemony flavor that can complement many dishes. Although predominantly associated with flavoring teas and ice creams, the chopped leaves of this plant can add depth to a number of dishes including fish, chicken, fruits, salads, egg dishes and desserts.

Lemon balm goes well with other herbs and spices including parsley, thyme, rosemary, allspice and mint.

Lemon balm works great with both sweet and tangy dishes and it's leaves can also be a nice garnish for any plate. Its tangy flavor is perfect for marinades and sauces as well as herb butters and can even lend interesting zest to stuffings.

Microwave Lemon Balm Vanilla Pudding

Ingredients:

- 1/2 cup sugar
- 1/4 cup corn starch
- 2 cups milk
- 2 eggs, slightly beaten in a medium sized bowl
- 2 tablespoons butter
- 1 teaspoon vanilla
- 3 tablespoons fresh lemon balm finely minced

Preparation:

Whisk together the cornstarch and sugar in a medium sized glass bowl.

Stir the milk in slowly.

Cook in microwave on high power until thickened - about 5 - 7 minutes. Stirring every 2 minutes. Some microwaves might take longer, just keep checking every minute or so after 5 minutes. Don't let it "boil" or it will be ruined!

Beat half of the hot mixture into the egg mixture then pour that into the hot mixture and mix thoroughly.

Microwave on high for 1 - 2 1/2 minutes until very thick. Stir every 45 seconds.

Stir in butter, vanilla and lemon balm.

Pour into individual dishes, cover and refrigerate.

Lemon Balm Cookies

Ingredients:

- 1 cup butter
- 1 cup sugar
- 1 egg
- 2 2/3 cups flour
- 1/4 teaspoon salt
- 2 teaspoons vanilla extract
- 6 lemon balm leaves minced or ground with mortar and pestle

Preparation:

In a large bowl, cream the sugar and butter until fluffy.

Beat in the egg, vanilla and lemon balm.

Whisk the flour and salt together and then add to the other ingredients.

Cover dough and chill for an hour.

Preheat oven to 400F.

Drop dough by spoonfuls onto chilled, un-greased cookie sheets and press into flat cookies.

Bake 8 - 10 minutes.

LICORICE

Plant Family: Leguminosae

Where Grown: Originating in Turkey and the Middle East, it is now grown in Southern Europe, Asia, Western U.S. and the Middle East

Parts Used: Roots

Other Names: Sweetroot, Sweetwood

Licorice is a sweet herb that has been used in flavorings as well as medicinal remedies since ancient times. As a sweetener, it is very powerful and actually contains a compound that is 50 times sweeter than sugar.

The plant is a perennial that can grow from three to seven feet tall with an extensive root system. It is the roots that are used for both cooking and healing. These tough woody roots are brown on the outside and yellow on the inside and about the width of a pencil.

Licorice plants can be grown from a cutting or a seed. It takes several years to reach maturity so plan on having the plant in your garden for quite a while. They will do best in a temperate climate with sandy soil close to a source of water. After three or four years of growth, the licorice plant should be harvested and the roots set aside for drying in the sun or under low heat. The rest of the plant is not used and can be discarded.

Licorice root has long been used for a variety of health problems and the Roman naturalist Theophrastus wrote about its uses for asthma and other lung disorders as far back as 280 B.C.. In China, it was first mentioned in the 1st century A.D. where it was also used for asthma, coughs and gastric problems.

The root itself is too tough to include in most food dishes, but some cultures do chew on it as a natural breath freshener after meals.

Health Benefits

Licorice is a powerful expectorant as well as a diuretic, an anti-inflammatory and also has soothing effects for mucous membranes. As such, it is used in treating problems of the lungs such as coughing and asthma.

Another interesting use for licorice is in treating peptic ulcers. There's been a couple of studies that have shown that Deglycyrrhizinated licorice combined with antacids have been effective in treating peptic ulcers but it is not known if the licorice alone would have been just as effective. Another study treated 100 patients with a licorice root fluid extract for 6 weeks. These patients had not been able to improve their condition with conventional medications. In 22 of the patients the ulcers disappeared completely and 90% of the participants saw some improvement.

Topical ointments or gels with licorice can also improve some skin conditions such as eczema and canker sores.

A recent study also showed that licorice may discourage plaque from forming in your arteries which can aid in the prevention of heart disease.

Licorice is shown to have hundreds of potentially healing substances within it and can be used for a variety of ailments. It also can enhance your immunity because it is been shown to boost the levels of interferon which is an immune system chemical. It also is a powerful antioxidant and contains phytoestrogens that could be helpful in treating menopausal symptoms. Other compounds in licorice may also help stop the growth of bacteria and viruses which can make it effective in treating flu's and colds.

Licorice root does promote water retention so people that have hypertension or are using diuretics should avoid it as should people with diabetes or cirrhosis of the liver.

Culinary Uses

Licorice root has a pleasant anise flavor and can be used to enhance many foods especially baked goods, but the root itself is too tough to actually include in any of your cooking. The best use is to steep it in some sort of liquid to impart the flavor for use in your dishes. You will find most recipes include a licorice root extract for flavoring, or you can boil the licorice root yourself in water and then strain out the tough roots and use the water for flavoring.

Licorice Root Tea

Ingredients:

- 3 cups water
- 1 1/2 teaspoons dried licorice root
- 1/2 cinnamon stick
- 1 teaspoon dried chamomile flowers
- 3 teaspoons honey

Preparation:

Bring water to a boil over high heat.

Stir in licorice, cinnamon and chamomile.

Remove from heat and let steep for 10 minutes.

Strain out the dried herbs.

Add the honey.

Pour into cups and serve. Can be served as a hot tea or cooled for an hour and then served over ice as an ice tea.

MACE

Plant Family: Myristicaceae

Where Grown: Originating in Indonesia, it is now cultivated in Sri Lanka, Grenada, Indonesia and Madagascar

Parts Used: Outer covering of the nut

Other Names: Blade Mace

Originating from the spice Islands of Indonesia, mace was a highly popular spice in the 15th and 17th centuries but isn't really used too much today even though it's strong taste and heat is perfect for adding depth to both sweet and savory dishes.

Most people don't know that mace is actually the covering of the outer shell of nutmeg. Interestingly enough, the *Myristica fragrans* tree yields both these spices - it produces an apricot like fruit and nutmeg is actually the kernel of this fruit. The nutmeg kernel or seed is encased in a hard covering which is covered in a membrane. The membrane, which is bright red and rubbery is mace. This lacy membrane is cut away by hand and laid out to dry. Once dried it is cut into blades or ground up and used as the spice we know as mace.

Both nutmeg and mace were used as food flavors in ancient Asia. In Rome, they were preferred as editions to alcoholic drinks. During medieval times, mace was frequently added to foods along with nutmeg and cinnamon.

Health Benefits

Mace has traditionally been used to relieve stomach upset such as vomiting and diarrhea. In Ayurvedic medicine, it was used in aphrodisiac formulas along with other herbs. Mace can also help stimulate digestion and relieve gas and bloating.

Although safe to be eaten in the small amounts that it is used in foods, mace can be toxic in high doses and can cause over excitement and even hallucinations so care should be taken with this herb. One should never eat more than 3 g of mace which is way more than you would ever use in any prepared food.

Mace contains many nutrients including zinc, manganese, copper, magnesium, chromium, phosphorus, calcium, niacin, riboflavin, thiamine and carotene.

Culinary Uses

Though mace is typically sold ground into powder, you may be able to buy the blades and if you do, look for ones that are still a bit rubbery as the brittle ones are considerably older and less flavorful. In recipes, you can substitute 1 teaspoon of ground mace for a tablespoon of mace blades.

Mace is a warming spice and much like nutmeg lends a warm, somewhat spicy quality to your food. It can be used in sweet or savory dishes but be sure to use it in moderation as the flavor is very strong.

Mace goes particularly well with milk dishes as well as chocolate and can lend an interesting zip to sweet potatoes and regular mashed potatoes.

Baked Squash and Apples

Ingredients:

- 1/2 cup light brown sugar, packed
- 1 tablespoon all purpose flour
- 1 teaspoon salt
- 1/2 teaspoon ground mace
- 1/4 cup butter, melted
- 2 pounds butternut squash cut into 1/2 inch chunks
- 2 large apples cut into 1/2 inch chunks

Preparation:

Preheat oven to 350F

Stir together everything but the squash and apples.

Spread squash and apple pieces in un-greased 9 x 13 baking dish.

Top with sugar mixture.

Cover and bake for 60 minutes or until squash is tender.

Lemon Mace Cookies

Ingredients:

- 1/4 teaspoon mace
- 2 cups flour, sifted
- 2 teaspoons baking powder
- 1/2 teaspoon salt
- 2 eggs
- 2/3 cup canola oil
- 3/4 cup white sugar
- 1/4 cup brown sugar
- 2 teaspoons lemon peel, grated
- 1 teaspoon lemon juice

Preparation:

Preheat over to 400F.

In a large bowl, sift together the mace, flour and baking powder.

Add the remaining ingredients and beat well.

Drop by teaspoons onto greased cookie sheets

Bake for 8 - 10 minutes.

MARJORAM

Plant Family: Mint (Lamiaceae)

Where Grown: Originating in North Africa, it is now grown throughout the Mediterranean, North America and Western Asia

Parts Used: Leaves

Other Names: Joy Of The Mountains, Pot Marjoram, Sweet Marjoram, Knotted Marjoram

Marjoram is an aromatic herb that has been used for thousands of years. Although it's not one of the most popular herbs used in cooking today, it was a staple herb back in ancient times. This cousin of oregano has a similar flavor but sweeter and much more delicate.

Popular in Greek and Italian cuisine, this herb has been used as a cold remedy and for preserving foods since ancient times. It was also placed on tombs to help the departed spirit find peace. This herb was said to be a favorite of Aphrodite and was used to symbolize love honor and happiness for bridal couples in the Middle Ages.

At one time, marjoram was an ingredient in snuff as well as a preservative in beer.

Despite its subtle, delicate flavor, marjoram can add great depth to a hearty stew or soup and goes well with meat dishes.

Marjoram is a tender perennial best grown in zones 7-9. It likes a rich, slightly alkaline soil and a lot of sunlight. Its leaves are very aromatic and small in size with a grayish green color and a fine fuzz on them. When dried, the fuzz looks like dust on the leaf.

The plant is harvested as it begins to flower and the leaves are dried or used fresh. The flowers can be used to distill the essential oils of the plant.

Health Benefits

Despite its subtle flavor, marjoram is considered to have the most fragrant essential oil and is widely used in aromatherapy as well as a massage oil. It is said to be able to help fight asthma, stomach and digestive issues and headaches. It can also be used as a steaming inhalation to help clear the sinuses, relieve laryngitis and soothe the vocal chords.

The leaves can have benefits as a decongestant and have been used to treat bronchitis, sinusitis and colds. It is more calming than oregano and can be a good tonic for the nervous system.

Marjoram can also help treat digestive issues such as flatulence, nausea indigestion and even loss of appetite. It is a member of the mint family and can be helpful in soothing digestive upsets including colic.

Marjoram has anti-inflammatory properties so it can be effecting in helping to relieve aches and pains as well as treat bruises, stiff joints and even toothaches. Also being an anti-spasmodic, it can be used to treat cramps and painful menstruation problems. Since it stimulates sweating, it can be helpful in removing toxins through the skin as well as to reduce fevers.

This herb has high levels of Vitamin C, beta carotene, Vitamin A, lutein and zeaxanthin and is one of the richest herbal sources of vitamin K providing over 500% of your RDA. It is also loaded with minerals like calcium, manganese, potassium, iron, copper, zinc and magnesium.

Culinary Uses

Unlike many herbs, marjoram has more flavor when dried. You should add it during the final moments of cooking because it will lose flavor once heated. Cooks use it in both fresh and dried form. Fresh leaves are good when used in flavoring salads, stews, soups and marinades as well as combined with eggs.

Dried marjoram is often used in Italian and Greek cuisine and goes quite well with spinach, tomatoes, potatoes and carrots. It can be combined with other herbs such as thyme, parsley, bay leaf and tarragon.

Roasted Shrimp with Marjoram

Ingredients:

- 2 pounds large shrimp
- 1 cup olive oil
- 2 tablespoons chopped fresh marjoram (or 2 teaspoons dried)
- 1 teaspoon lemon zest
- 2 teaspoons lemon juice
- 2 teaspoons kosher salt
- 2 cloves garlic, minced
- Black pepper to taste

Preparation:

Preheat over to 425F.

Wash and devein the shrimp.

Mix the ingredients in a large bowl, put shrimp in the bowl and toss to coat. If you want you can marinate the shrimp for up to 4 hours.

Spread the shrimp on a baking sheet and cook for 3 to 5 minutes until shells turn pink and the shrimp is no longer translucent.

Savory Beef Stew

Ingredients:

- 2 lbs stew beef in 1" cubes
- 2 tablespoons all purpose flour
- 1/2 teaspoon black pepper
- 2 tablespoons olive oil
- 3 cloves garlic, minced
- 1 bay leaf
- 1/2 teaspoon marjoram dried (crushed)
- 1/2 teaspoon thyme dried (crushed)
- 1/2 teaspoon rosemary dried (crushed)
- 1 3/4 cups beef broth
- 3 cups carrots cut to 1" slices
- 10 whole small red potatoes

Preparation:

Heat oil in saucepan on medium heat.

Season beef with flour and pepper, add to saucepan and cook until brown. Stir often.

Add herbs, bay leaf and garlic and stir well.

Add broth, cover heat to a boil, lower heat and simmer 45 minutes.

Add carrots and potatoes, heat to a boil, turn heat to low, cover and cook for 30 minutes or until beef is done.

Remove bay leaf before serving.

MINT

Plant Family: Mint (Lamiaceae)

Where Grown: Originating in the Northern Mediterranean it is now grown worldwide.

Parts Used: Leaves

Mint is an aromatic perennial and one of the most popular herbs as well as one of the easiest to grow. Originating in the Mediterranean, it is now grown throughout the world and enjoyed in all types of cuisine. There are actually many different types of mint plants most of which are perennial and spread underground through runners but can also be propagated through seeds or cuttings rooted in water.

Some species of mint grow faster than others but beware that they can be invasive in your garden so be careful of which types you plant. Mint can be a great companion plant because it repels many garden pests and insects. It can also be grown in a pot both outdoors or inside making it a favorite windowsill herb.

In ancient times, mint was a symbol of hospitality and it was the Romans who introduced it to Europe where its use spread quickly. In the West, we think of mint as an herb to use in sweet dishes but in Mediterranean regions it is included in a lot of savory dishes as well.

You can harvest your mint leaves at any time by simply plucking them off the plant so it is great to have some plants growing in the garden or on the windowsill where you can just reach over for a fresh supply any time you want. It's best to use the leaves right away or store them in a plastic bag in the fridge for a couple of days.

Health Benefits

Mint tea has been a remedy for digestive troubles for centuries. It is an anti spasmodic that is said to help with stomach cramps and relieve symptoms of heartburn, Irritable Bowel Syndrome and colitis. The oils in mint are also said to help relieve the pain of hemorrhoids.

Of course, we all know that mint makes a good breath freshener and it is used today in many breath mints, toothpaste and mouthwashes.

Mint is very aromatic and it is said that crushed, fresh mint leaves can help get rid of headache as well as nausea. This strong aroma can also help with coughing and respiratory disorders. Much like eucalyptus it can help open up the bronchi and lungs giving relief from coughs and colds as well as asthma. In addition, mint is a good relaxant and can help relax the bronchial tubes in asthma patients.

Mint contains menthol which makes it a great remedy for sinus trouble when inhaled. You could also use the oils topically as a rub for sore muscles and also to help treat minor burns, bites and skin irritations.

Mint is a powerful antioxidant and contains Vitamin C, Vitamin A Vitamin B12, folic acid, riboflavin, copper, calcium, zinc, fluoride, iron, manganese, phosphorus, potassium and selenium.

Culinary Uses

Mint is a very versatile and refreshing herb and can be used in both savory and sweet dishes. It goes particularly well with lamb as evidenced by the fact that mint jelly is a staple with many lamb dishes.

For most cooking purposes, spearmint is the variety that is used. It goes well with cooked vegetables and is a great refreshing addition to salads. In the Middle East it is used in both fresh and dried form in dishes with meats and stuffed vegetables. It is a staple in tabbouleh and also common in Thai and Vietnamese soups and salads.

Peppermint goes exceptionally well with dark chocolate (if you've ever had a York Peppermint Patty, you know what I mean) and is perfect for desserts due to its fresh, cooling flavor. It is the menthol that gives it this icy feeling and more often than not a peppermint extract is used for flavoring desserts as opposed to the fresh herb.

Mint & Ginger Haddock

Ingredients:

- 1 bunch of mint
- 2" of ginger peeled and minced
- 1 tablespoon vegetable oil
- 1/2 teaspoon salt
- 1/2 teaspoon black pepper
- 2 pounds haddock fillets

Preparation:

Preheat oven to 350F.

Rinse fish and pat dry.

Arrange fish side by side in baking dish. Be sure not to overlap too much of the fish - it should be one layer.

Mix mint, ginger, oil, salt and pepper in a food processor or blender until it becomes a smooth paste. You may have to add some water to get this to happen.

Spread the paste over the fish.

Bake 20 - 30 minutes or until fish is opaque and flakes easily.

Mint Yogurt Dressing

Ingredients:

- 1/4 cup mint leaves, chopped
- 1/2 cup yogurt
- 1 clove garlic, minced
- Salt and pepper to taste

Preparation:

Combine all the ingredients in a small bowl. If you want a thinner consistency like for a salad dressing then add some lemon juice. This makes a great dip for vegetables or fruit or dressing for any dish!

MUSTARD

Plant Family: Cruciferae

Where Grown: Originating in Northern Europe, Asia and India, mustard seeds are now widely grown across central latitudes.

Parts Used: Seeds

Mustard seeds which yield the condiment we associate so closely with food was actually first used as a medicinal plant. The Greek scientist Pythagoras used mustard to treat scorpion stings and Hippocrates used it in a variety of poultices and other healing medicines.

Mustard is the second most used spice in the US (surpassed only by pepper) and it goes perfectly on all kinds of meats, seafood, poultry and in dips and dressings. Mustard plants grow in temperate climates and yield small pods that are filled with these tiny seeds. There are over 40 different types of mustard plants but only 3 main types of seeds are typically used for cooking.

The white seeds which make the bright yellow mustard that we are used to are the ones that typically grow in the Mediterranean area. Brown seeds are brown in color and are often found in Americanized Chinese cooking. Black seeds come from the Middle East and are used in Middle Eastern dishes.

These days, most people buy mustard in a prepared solution but you can also get the seeds whole or ground up in powdered form. There are a ton of different specialty mustards as well is flavored mustards that you can use to add zip to any number of dishes.

Health Benefits

Because they are high in mucilage, mustard seeds can be used as a laxative as well as an aid to digestion. They also have anti-septic and anti-fungal properties. Their anti-inflammatory properties make them a candidate for treatment of rheumatoid arthritis and asthma.

Mustard seeds contain high amounts of glucosinolates which have been studied for their anti-cancer effects. In animal studies, these glucosinolates have shown to inhibit the growth of cancer cells especially in the gastrointestinal tract and colon.

One interesting health benefit of consuming mustard seeds is that if they are eaten on a regular basis they may be beneficial for reducing the frequency of migraines.

Mustard seeds are high in antioxidants and also include a lot of selenium. In addition to that they have omega-3 fatty acids, Omega 6 fatty acids, phosphorus, potassium, magnesium and calcium.

It is also thought that rubbing mustard oil onto your scalp can help improve hair quality and prevent hair loss.

Culinary Uses

Mustard seeds and mustard powder can be used in a variety of dishes and as a tasty condiment. Dried mustard powder, when mixed with water, goes through an enzymatic process that makes it hotter and more pungent than the power alone. The water temperature will dictate the amount of spiciness in the mustard. Hotter water will make the mustard more mild and colder water will make it spicier.

Mustard can add a little zip to your mayonnaise as well as to a salad dressing or vinaigrette. Mustard can work as an emulsifier to stabilize two liquid ingredients that don't blend well such as oil and water.

You can buy mustard powder ready for use or buy the seeds and grind them yourself. Storing them in a cool dry place will help keep the flavor longer.

Mustard Potato Salad

Ingredients:

- 3 Russet potatoes, peeled and cut into cubes
- 1 small onion, chopped
- 3 tablespoons sweet pickle relish
- 1/3 cup mayonnaise
- 1/3 cup yellow mustard
- Salt and pepper to taste

Preparation:

Put the potatoes in a large pot and cover with water - add a pinch of salt.

Boil potatoes until just tender, then drain and let cool.

Combine onion, relish, mayonnaise and mustard in a large bowl.

Add potatoes to the mixture and stir to coat. Refrigerate for 30 minutes or serve right away. Season with salt and pepper to taste.

Lemon Mustard Vinaigrette

Ingredients:

- 1/2 teaspoon prepared Dijon mustard
- 2 tablespoons lemon juice (fresh squeezed is best!)
- 4 tablespoons extra virgin olive oil
- 1/4 teaspoon salt

Preparation:

Mix lemon juice, salt and mustard in a bowl.

Drizzle in the olive oil and whisk continuously until ingredients are combined.

NUTMEG

Plant Family: Myristicaceae

Where Grown: Originating in the Banda Islands it is now also grown in Indonesia, Sri Lanka, Grenada and Madagascar.

Parts Used: Inner Nut

Nutmeg is historically one of the most costly spices and the spice that started the big spice race of the 15th century. It was prized in Medieval cuisine as a flavoring and also coveted for its medicinal properties. It was said to have been able to ward off the plague and, as you can imagine, became very popular if not for this reason than for many others.

Up until the 19th century, the Banda islands were the only place the tree that produces nutmeg was grown. In the Middle Ages, the Arabs traded nutmeg to the Venetians and would not reveal their source so that they could maintain a monopoly on the trade and charge the highest of prices. Needless to say, there were many expeditions to find the source of this popular spice.

The Myristica fragrans, an evergreen tree, is what produces nutmeg and the "nut" is actually the inner seed of a peach like fruit. The fruit itself is bitter and toxic but when split open, it reveals a pit that yields 2 different spices. This hard shelled pit is covered in a bright red, rubbery, lacy veil which is hand cut and turned into the spice mace. Inside the hard shell is the nutmeg "nut" itself.

Health Benefits

Historically, nutmeg has been used to treat a variety of ailments but it is to be noted that it is the oils of the nut that have the most beneficial healing properties and those oils are present in the whole nut only but not really in the ground or powdered nutmeg that you buy in the grocery store for baking. So, if you want to reap the most health benefits of this tasty spice then you will want to buy the whole nut and grind it yourself.

Nutmeg has anti-inflammatory properties so it is traditionally used to treat inflammation such as joint problems and even asthma. It can also be used for stomach pain and is said to be a good liver and kidney tonic to aid in removing toxins from the body. In addition to that, it is said that nutmeg oil can be helpful in dissolving kidney stones as well as relieving kidney infections,

Nutmeg also has strong antibacterial properties and is particularly good at killing cavity causing bacteria in the mouth as well as treating bad breath, gum problems and toothaches.

The ancient Romans used it as a brain tonic and modern studies reveal that nutmeg contains a compound called myristicin which is shown to improve memory as well as inhibit an enzyme in the brain that contributes to Alzheimer's disease. It can also help limit fatigue and stress as well as help improve your concentration.

Nutmeg also has relaxing properties and can be used as a sleep aid.

Nutmeg can be toxic if taken in high doses so you want to be sure to limit your dosage to one nut or less than 1 teaspoon at a time.

Culinary Uses

Nutmeg is one of those fragrant holiday spices that is associated with sweet and spicy dishes, pies and puddings, custard and even eggnog. It complements egg dishes quite nicely and can even work well with vegetables like spinach broccoli and eggplant.

In Indian cuisine it is used in sweets. In European cuisine it can be found in a lot of potato dishes and processed meats. In Middle Eastern dishes it is often seen with lamb. Japanese curry powder includes nutmeg as one of the ingredients.

Nutmeg produces a warm spicy flavor that is best tasted from a freshly grated nut. There are graters specifically designed for this and you can buy a whole nutmeg then take it out to grate it as needed. Unlike many spices nutmeg will store for quite some time so you can just cover up the nut and put it in the fridge then bring it out for fresh grated nutmeg the next time you are making a recipe that calls for it.

Spicy Banana Bread

Ingredients:

- 1/4 teaspoon ground nutmeg
- 1/2 teaspoon ground cinnamon
- 2 1/4 cups whole wheat flour
- 3/4 teaspoon baking soda
- 1/4 teaspoon salt
- 3 ripe bananas mashed up
- 1/4 cup plain yogurt
- 1/4 cup honey
- 2 eggs
- 1/3 cup coconut oil (or canola oil, but coconut is healthier!)
- 1 teaspoon vanilla

Preparation:

Preheat oven to 350F

In a large bowl, whisk flour, baking soda, salt, cinnamon and nutmeg.

In another bowl, combine bananas, yogurt, eggs, honey, oil and vanilla.

Add banana mixture to the flour, folding in until blended but do not overmix.

Pour batter into a large loaf pan.

Bake about 40 minutes or until a toothpick inserted in the center comes out clean.

Cauliflower Nutmeg Soup

Ingredients:

- 1 Cauliflower, cut into pieces
- 2 pints vegetable stock
- 3 1/2 oz heavy cream
- 2 oz butter
- 2 onions, chopped
- 1 teaspoon nutmeg, freshly ground
- Salt and pepper to taste

Preparation:

Melt butter in pan and saute onions and cauliflower until golden brown.

Add the vegetable stock and bring to a boil.

Reduce heat, add nutmeg, cover and simmer for 20 minutes.

Transfer to a blender, add cream and blend until smooth. Be careful of the hot liquid!

ONION

Plant Family: Alliaceae

Where Grown: Originating in Central Asia, they now are grown most anywhere.

Parts Used: Bulb

It's not every herb that can bring tears to your eyes, but the onion can. Of course I'm not referring to its wonderful taste but to the problem that happens when you try to cut them. Onions have very strong sulfur compound and when you cut into them the allicin activates a sulfur like gas which wafts up into your eyes causing that familiar tearing. Of course, it is this allicin that also gives it some of its healthy properties and pungent taste.

Onions have been eaten and cultivated since prehistoric times and have even been mentioned in texts translated from Mesopotamia. They appear quite frequently in Egyptian tombs and ancient Egyptian art dating them as far back as 3200 BC.

Ancient Grecian athletes ate lots of onions because they were thought to lighten the blood and Roman gladiators were rubbed down with onion to firm the muscles. In the Middle Ages, onions were so revered that people would pay their rent with them and give them as gifts.

In 1492 Christopher Columbus thought he introduced the onion to America but it turns out that onions were already growing throughout North America and Native Americans were eating them in a variety of different ways.

Health Benefits

Onions contain anti-inflammatory and antioxidant properties and are thought to help reduce cholesterol and may even help lessen the risk of cancer.

In some parts of the world onions are used to heal blisters and boils and are applied topically to the affected area. Raw onion is also reputed to help reduce the swelling from bee stings.

Onions contain compounds that destroy osteoclasts which break down bone so it is thought that eating a lot of onions could be beneficial to women who are at risk of osteoporosis.

Onions have been used traditionally to heal sore throats in India and an American chemist noted that some of the chemicals found in onions would have the potential to alleviate or prevent sore throats.

Onions have a lot of vitamins and minerals such as vitamin C, B6, biotin, chromium, dietary fiber, calcium, folic acid, vitamin B1 and vitamin K. They also are a good source of quercitin which is a very powerful antioxidant that has been linked to inhibiting stomach cancer. Quercitin also helps lower bad cholesterol, raise good cholesterol and thin the blood. It is thought that a half of a raw onion a day can help prevent blood clots, fight bronchitis and asthma and ward off infections.

Onions also contain amino acids that are said to be good at detoxifying your body from heavy metal and can help leach mercury, cadmium lead out of your body. Eating onions can help lower your blood sugar and their strong antibacterial powers can kill off many disease causing pathogens including salmonella and E. coli.

Culinary Uses

Onions are one of the staple foods in any kitchen and are used in a variety of dishes as both an herb and a vegetable. They are very versatile and can be used in varying amounts from just a few tablespoons to a few onions and even make their debut as a main ingredient in dishes such as French Onion Soup and Steak and Onions.

Onions taste good steamed, boiled, roasted, sautéed, baked, fried, braised or grilled and, of course, even raw in salads.

There are many different varieties of onions to be used depending on your needs. The yellow onions are the strongest and probably the most popular for cooking but they can be very strong to use raw. White onions are sweeter and red onions are mild being the best choice for salads or raw eating.

When using onions, one should take care to discard any that have a green stem growing as this can make them bitter.

Caramelized Onion Quiche

Ingredients:

- 9" unbaked pie crust (make your own or buy premade)
- 2 tablespoons olive oil
- 3 red onions
- 1 teaspoon balsamic vinegar
- 1/2 cup milk
- 1/2 cup heavy cream
- 3 eggs
- 1 1/2 cups swiss cheese, grated
- 1/8 teaspoon nutmeg
- Salt and pepper to taste

Preparation:

Preheat oven to 350F.

Cut onions into very thin slices.

Heat oil on medium in a heavy saucepan and add onions and sprinkle a little salt on them.

Cook, stirring occasionally, until the onions are translucent.

Reduce heat to medium low and cook for about 40 minutes until they are brown.

Add balsamic vinegar and cook until onions are caramelized - about 10 more minutes.

Layer the onions in the pie crust.

Add the cheese over the onions.

Mix the milk, cream, eggs, nutmeg, salt and pepper and pour over the cheese and onions.

Bake for about 30 minutes until just set in center.

French Onion Soup

Ingredients:

- 6 large yellow onions, thinly sliced
- Olive oil
- 1/4 teaspoon sugar
- 2 cloves garlic, minced
- 8 cups reduced sodium beef broth
- 1/2 cup dry white wine
- 1 bay leaf
- 3 sprigs of fresh thyme
- Salt and pepper to taste
- 8 slices toasted French baguette
- 1 1/2 cups grated Swiss Gruyere

Preparation:

Cover the bottom of a large sauce pan with olive oil and add onions.

Sauté on medium high heat until onions are browned (40 minutes or more) - add sugar after 10 minutes to help them caramelize.

Add garlic and sauté for 1 minute longer

Add stock, wine, bay leaf and thyme.

Cover and simmer for 30 minutes.

Discard bay leaf and season with salt and pepper to taste.

Ladle into oven proof soup bowls, cover with a slice of toast and sprinkle cheese on top then sit under broiler until cheese bubbles and starts to turn brown.

OREGANO

Plant Family: Mint (Lamiaceae)

Where Grown: Originating in the Mediterranean, it is grown in Egypt, Greece, Italy and Turkey.

Parts Used: Leaves

Other Names: Wild Marjoram

Oregano conjures up images of Italian meals and pizza sauce, but early use of this herb dates to the Assyrians as far back as 3000 BC. This aromatic herb with its pungent peppery taste can add zip to all kinds of savory dishes.

The Greeks love this herb and it is called "Mountain Joy" because it grows in great abundance on the mountain sides of the Mediterranean. When the Romans conquered Greece, they developed a liking for oregano as well and spread that throughout Europe. Though used for centuries in Europe, it wasn't until after World War II that it became popular in the United States when soldiers discovered it in the Italian campaign and brought it home to add zest to their pizza.

Ancient Greeks and Romans used oregano to treat headaches and asthma and also as an antidote to poison. In the Middle Ages, it was a prominent herb in rituals and ceremonies and was often worn around the neck as a charm for health and good luck. At night sometimes people wore it on their head to induce psychic dreams and it was thought that putting it around your house could protect you from evil.

Oregano can be used fresh or dried and is produced from a small shrub that grows as a perennial in warm climates and an annual in cold climates. The shrub has multiple stems with small grayish green leaves and pink or white flowers.

Health Benefits

Oregano has long been known for its disease preventing properties. Hippocrates used it as a antiseptic and to treat stomach and respiratory ailments and it is still used in Greece today to treat sore throats.

Oregano is an anti-spasmodic, an expectorant, a stimulant, a tonic and a carminative herb with properties that can help treat colds, the flu, fevers, indigestion and other forms of stomach upset. It is even thought that oregano can help with gallbladder secretion.

This herb has one of the highest antioxidant activities and is high in vitamin A, vitamin K, carotene, manganese, iron, vitamin E, calcium and tryptophan and also has a high volume of dietary fiber.

Culinary Uses

Oregano with its camphor-like taste can be used fresh or dried. The dried version can be more flavorful and is mostly known for its use on pizza here in the U.S.

It is the staple herb in Italian-American cooking being added to most marinara sauces, but in Italy it is also used on vegetable, meat and fish dishes. It is also used in other cuisines especially Mediterranean cuisine. Turkish cooks use it to flavor meats and the Greeks like to add it to salads.

If you are substituting fresh oregano for dried use twice as much as the recipe calls for. Fresh oregano leaves will stay good in the refrigerator for a couple of weeks when sealed in a plastic bag.

Lemon Garlic Chicken With Oregano

Ingredients:

* 4 pounds chicken parts (thighs and legs are best but breasts could work too)
* 1/4 cup fresh lemon juice
* 1/4 cup fresh oregano, finely chopped
* 2 cloves garlic, crushed
* 2 teaspoons black pepper
* 2 tablespoons salt
* 3 tablespoons melted butter

Preparation:

In a small bowl, whisk lemon juice, oregano, garlic, pepper and salt to combine.

Pour marinade into a gallon size freezer bag and add chicken to the bag. Make sure all the chicken is coated with the marinade and let marinate in refrigerator for 2 hours.

Preheat over to 425F.

Place chicken in single layer in a large baking dish. Save the marinade.

Brush chicken with melted butter.

After 25 minutes, baste the chicken with the rest of the marinade.

Bake until chicken is cooked through - about 30 minutes more (around 55 minutes total cooking time).

Pizza Sauce

Ingredients:

- 3 tablespoons olive oil
- 3 cloves garlic, crushed
- 1 can tomato puree
- 1 can crushed tomatoes
- 2 teaspoons Italian seasoning
- 2 teaspoons dried oregano
- 2 teaspoons dried thyme
- 2 teaspoons dried basil
- 1/2 teaspoon crushed red pepper flakes
- 1 tablespoon brown sugar

Preparation:

- Sauté garlic and oil in a large saucepan on low until golden.
- Add the rest of the ingredients, raise heat and bring to a boil.
- Reduce heat and simmer uncovered, stirring occasionally until the sauce reaches it's desired thickness (about 30 minutes).

PAPRIKA

Plant Family: Nightshade (Solanaceae)

Where Grown: Originating in South America it is grown extensively in Hungary and Spain.

Parts Used: Fruit

Other Names: Pimenton

Made from dried and crushed sweet red peppers and chili peppers, paprika is a traditional spice used in South American and Hungarian cuisine.

Originally a tropical plant that grew only in South America, it has now been cultivated to grow in cooler temperatures as well. The plant is a herbaceous annual with white flowers that produce the fruit (i.e peppers) that are eventually dried and crushed into powder. The peppers are green when they start out but ripen to red, purple or brown. Only the red ones are used for paprika.

While in the U.S. paprika is not one of the more common spices, it is actually the 4th most consumed spice because it is used in many blended spices including chili powders, barbecue rubs and seasoned salts.

Paprika is known for giving foods a reddish orange color and, in fact, is used in many processed foods as a natural coloring.

The taste of the spice can range from sweet to savory to spicy depending on the origin of the blend.

Paprika is a powerful antioxidant and is loaded with vitamin C. In fact it has 9 times as much vitamin C as a tomato and 7 times as much as orange. It is also rich in the carotenoids which can help protect against cancer, heart disease and are well known for protecting the eyes. The high amount of vitamin C also helps your body absorb iron.

Paprika also contains capsaicin which gives it its anti-inflammatory properties and also makes it a good topical treatment for treating any inflammation due to sprains, bruises and even arthritis.

The natural antibacterial properties of paprika can help control bacteria such as salmonella and E. coli and, while it won't kill them off entirely, it might help to slow the growth of them which can help reduce the effects of food poisoning from this type of bacteria.

Paprika is also a stimulant that can help increase circulation as well as normalize blood pressure. It can be helpful in treating digestive problems because it can help boost saliva production and normalize stomach acids.

Be sure to buy naturally dried paprika as the commercial drying processes can leach away the vitamins and nutrients that make it so healthy

Culinary Uses

Paprika is closely associated with Hungarian cuisine especially Hungarian goulash but it can be found in many other cuisines and goes great in soups, stews and casseroles. It can be found in a lot of spiced sausages and is a popular garnish on deviled eggs, hors d'oeuvres and salads.

Paprika can also be an emulsifier that can help bind olive oil and vinegar in salad dressings.

Paprika is used extensively in commercial foods, in fact if you buy any foods that are red or orange in color and list "natural coloring" on the label it's a pretty sure bet that they contain paprika.

This spice does not keep well, so buy it in small amounts and use quickly because the taste, as well as the health benefits, of paprika do diminish quite a bit over time.

Paprika BBQ Rub

Ingredients:

- 1/4 cup paprika
- 1/4 cup brown sugar
- 1/4 cup garlic salt
- 2 tablespoons black pepper

Preparation:

Mix all ingredients in a bowl. Use to marinate chicken, beef or pork. Store in a cool dry place.

Chicken Paprikash

Ingredients:

- 2 pounds boneless, skinless chicken breasts
- 2 teaspoons salt
- 2 tablespoons unsalted butter
- 3 large yellow onions, thinly sliced
- 2 tablespoons sweet paprika
- 1 teaspoon hot paprika
- 1 cup chicken broth
- 1/2 cup sour cream
- Black pepper to taste

Preparation:

Melt butter in a large sauté pan.

Salt chicken and place in pan, cook on each side until browned.

Remove chicken and set aside.

Add onions to sauté pan, cook on medium stirring to scrape up the browned bits from the chicken. Cook until onions are golden, about 7 minutes.

Add both the sweet and hot paprika and the black pepper and stir.

Add the chicken broth and stir, scraping up the browned bits from the bottom.

Place chicken on top of onion mixture, cover and simmer on low for 25 minutes or until chicken is cooked through.

Remove from heat and stir in sour cream.

PARSLEY

Plant Family: Parsley (Umbelliferia)

Where Grown: Originating in Southern Europe, it is grown pretty much everywhere now.

Parts Used: Leaves

Almost anyone who has eaten in a restaurant will recognize parsley, the bright green leafy garnished that you find on most dishes, but what you probably don't realize is this nutritious herb shouldn't be left on the plate with your scraps because you can enjoy a variety of health benefits by eating even a small amount.

This biennial herb was known for its medicinal properties way before it was ever used in cooking. The ancient Greeks used it in burial rituals as well as in wreath like crowns for winners of sports events. In medial times it was worn around the neck or placed on tables to reduce food odor and was also used as a poison antidote. Hippocrates used it for a variety of health reasons.

This bright green plant grows pretty much anywhere around the world and is a biennial in temperate climates and an annual in subtropical climates. It is easy to grow in the garden as well as to grow in pots indoors. There are over 100 different varieties but what we most recognize are the curly parsley and the flat leaf or Italian parsley.

For growing your own parsley, you want to make sure you have moist, rich soil. The plant grows to about 2 feet tall and has small white or greenish yellow flowers. The leaves are best used fresh. Dried parsley is sold in many stores and can be added to soups and sauces, but when the fresh herb is so readily available why would you want to use dried?

This plant makes a great companion plant in the garden because it attracts wasps and flies which will then protect the other nearby plants from some garden pests. Swallowtail butterflies use it as a host plant so you might want to watch out for their caterpillars. Goldfinches like to eat the seeds that are produced by the plant.

Health Benefits

Traditionally, parsley is used for digestion and kidney problems. It can help treat kidney stones as well as gallstones and reduce urine retention as it is a powerful diuretic. It is also said to be a good tonic herb for the liver and spleen.

Parsley is also said to help improve function of the adrenal glands, optic nerve, brain and nervous system. It is a powerful tonic for capillaries and arterioles and is thought to help reduce cardiovascular disease as it can help maintain elasticity as well as cleanse the blood and reduce clotting. The high levels of vitamin B 9 help to lower homocysteine levels which can help lessen the risk of clogged arteries, heart attack and stroke.

It is a powerful anti-inflammatory and loaded with antioxidants being high in vitamin C, vitamin A, vitamin K, vitamin B, manganese, copper, iodine, calcium, potassium and various flavonoids.

It has twice as much iron as spinach and 2 tablespoons have 153% of the RDA of vitamin K which is very good for keeping a healthy immune system as well as healthy bones.

With all these antioxidant vitamins and flavonoids, it's easy to see how parsley can have a powerful boost on the immune system.

Parsley also contains compounds that help relax stiff joints and can be used as a topical remedy for bruising.

Parsley is a very powerful herb and should be used with caution. It is perfectly safe to eat in regular food amounts but pregnant women should take care not to eat it in excess. When used as a juice, one should not have more than 2 ounces at a time.

Culinary Uses

Used extensively as a garnish, parsley also makes its presence known in salads, soups, sauces and homemade juices for health. It is great to add to mayonnaise and other dressings as well as to rice dishes, stocks and mashed potatoes. You might even consider adding it to meatballs or burgers or serving it over fish. The massive health benefits make it a great herb to add to any dish that you can and it really does go well with most anything. In fact, you can even include it in stuffing, use it in sauces (especially pesto sauce), sprinkle it over seafood and add it into butter for spreading on bread.

Parsley is used often in European, American and Middle Eastern cooking. It is best used fresh and when the leaves are chewed they can make a great breath freshener which is another reason, of course, to have it as a garnish on your plate.

Parsley Pesto

Ingredients:

- 2 cups flat leaf parsley
- 1 teaspoon extra virgin olive oil
- 2 tablespoons pine nuts, toasted
- 1 1/2 tablespoons Parmigiano-Reggiano cheese grated
- 1/4 teaspoon salt

Preparation:

Combine ingredients in food processor until smooth.

Parsley Salad

Ingredients:

- 1 large bunch curly parsley, chopped
- 1/2 cup basil leaves, chopped
- 3 tomatoes diced
- 1 teaspoon minced garlic
- 1/2 lemon
- 3/4 cup olive oil
- 3 oz Parmigiano-Reggiano cheese, grated
- 2 pinches salt
- 2 pinches teaspoon freshly ground black pepper

Preparation:

In a large bowl, combine parsley, basil, tomatoes and garlic. Toss to mix.

Squeeze lemon over the salad, sprinkle olive oil, salt and pepper over salad. Toss to mix.

Grate that Parmigiano-Reggiano over the top.

PEPPERCORN

Plant Family: Pepper (Piperaceae)

Where Grown: Originating in India, now grown in India, Indonesia and South America

Parts Used: Fruits

Peppercorns are perhaps the world's most popular spice and one that has been coveted since ancient times. I am referring to the hard black berry that is ground up to create the black pepper that you are used to seeing in a shaker on the dinner table.

Possibly the oldest spice, peppercorns were cultivated as far back as 1000 B.C.. They were once considered as valuable as gold and up until as recently as the 19th century were a luxury only the rich could afford. Peppercorns were so precious that ancient Romans used them to pay their taxes and they were even used as paychecks for Centurions.

Today, pepper is the 3rd most added ingredient in recipes trailing only water and salt and counts for 25% of the world's spice trade.

Peppercorns are the seed berries of the *piper nigrum* tree. There are actually 4 different types; black, green, white and red but the most well-known and most widely used is the black which is the one we use for cooking as well as placing in shakers on the table. The green is the unripe berry which is usually sold freeze-dried, the white has less bite to it and is used in more mellow culinary dishes and the red are sweet and mellow and hardly seen in the West.

We know pepper as a flavor enhancing spice but it was actually first used for its medicinal properties as a digestive stimulant and expectorant.

Pepper has another interesting use too - it can help repel insects. In fact, a mixture of 1 quart water to 1/2 teaspoon freshly ground pepper sprayed on plants or in your drawers can help repel silverfish, moths, ants, bugs and even roaches. Sprinkling it on the ground in the middle of insect trails can deter them from their march.

Health Benefits

Pepper is long been used as an expectorant and digestive stimulant as well as a topical treatment that can help relieve hives and skin problems

This spice stimulates the taste buds which helps the stomach produce the right amount of hydrochloric acid. This, in turn, ensures that food is properly digested and leaves the stomach on time which can help relieve heartburn. It also ensures that the food getting into your digestive tract is digested properly which helps to reduce gas, diarrhea and constipation. Pepper can also help stimulate the breakdown of fat cells.

Pepper has antiseptic properties and has also been used to treat tooth decay as well as swelling gums.

This tasty spice is loaded with compounds that have a variety of health promoting properties. It's also full of antioxidants, vitamins and minerals including selenium, B complex vitamins, beta-carotene, potassium, calcium, manganese, iron, zinc, magnesium, vitamin K and vitamin C.

People with stomach ulcers, ulcerative colitis and diverticulitis should avoid it.

Culinary Uses

One of the most versatile spices for savory cooking, pepper can be used in virtually every dish including marinades and even some sweet dishes. It is well-known for its use on the table, often found in shakers alongside salt where one can use it to individually flavor their dishes.

It is best to use pepper freshly ground so you want to buy the whole peppercorns and then grind them yourself as needed. When buying peppercorns look for dark large berries and avoid ones that have a dusty look. Peppercorns will stay good at room temperature virtually forever so you can store them right in your peppermill and have fresh ground pepper on demand anytime you want.

Black Pepper Garlic Shrimp

Ingredients:

- 3 pounds shrimp, deveined
- 4 tablespoons freshly ground black pepper
- 3 tablespoons garlic, chopped
- 8 tablespoons butter

Preparation:

Preheat oven to 450F.
Spread shrimp out in a shallow baking pan.

In a saucepan, melt butter and add garlic. Sauté for 5 minutes on medium-low (do not overcook).

Pour butter and garlic mixture over shrimp, toss to coat all sides.

Spread pepper over shrimp.

Bake until shrimp are no longer translucent, turning once (about 7 minutes).

Black Pepper Crusted Tuna Steaks

Ingredients:

- 1 1/2 teaspoon salt
- 4 tablespoons black pepper, freshly grated
- 2 tablespoons vegetable oil
- 4 Tuna steaks

Preparation:

Sprinkle the Tuna steaks with salt.

Coat the steaks on both sides with the pepper - press it in so that it "sticks" to make an evenly coated crust.

Heat a heavy skillet on medium-high and place the steaks in to sear.

Sear steaks for about 2 minutes to side or until cooked to desired done-ness.

ROSEMARY

Plant Family: Mint (Lamiaceae)

Where Grown: Native to the Mediterranean, it is also grown in Turkey, North Africa and North America

Parts Used: Leaves

Other Names: Old man

Rosemary is a woody perennial herb with needlelike leaves and white, pink, blue or purple flowers. It grows to be about 5 feet tall and has a very distinctive smell much like a cross between lavender and pine. It is both a decorative and fragrant plant which makes it a good ornamental plant for your garden that has its uses in the kitchen as well.

That being said, Rosemary may be a bit of a challenge to grow in your home garden. Don't try sowing it from seed because it will take you at least 3 years to get a viable plant. Instead you'll want to try to grow from a cutting or, better yet, just buy an already started plant at the garden store. You want to plant it in well-drained soil that gets full sun. Rosemary is one of the more drought resistant plants so it's good to grow in areas that do not get a lot of rain.

Traditionally, Rosemary is an herb that symbolizes remembrance which is quite appropriate because it can also help improve memory. In the middle Ages it was associated with wedding ceremonies and putting it under your pillow was said to stop nightmares. Scattering it outside the home was said to   keep witches at bay.

Rosemary has a variety of health benefits and its distinct fragrance can be recognized in many facial creams and toiletries. It was one of the first herbs to be distilled for its essential oil and is still used in commercial products today.

Health Benefits

Rosemary has been used for its health benefits since ancient times when it was used to relieve abdominal pain, insomnia, gout and nervousness. It is a powerful antiseptic, antidepressant, anti-inflammatory and antiviral herb.

Studies have shown that rosemary can enhance memory due to the carnosic acid which may help protect the brain from free radicals. This can also help reduce the risk of strokes and diseases like Alzheimer's.

Rosemary is said to help with depression as well as to refresh and energize the mind. It has a calming effect they can help reduce nervousness.

Recent research shows that Rosemary can help age-related skin damage. When applied topically it helps strengthen capillaries as well as rejuvenate the skin.

Rosemary contains caffeic acid and rosemarinic acid which are both potent antioxidants and anti inflammatories and thought to help reduce inflammation that can contribute to heart disease, liver disease and asthma.

Rosemary has been shown to be able to inactivate toxins and flush them from your body before they can do damage according to studies done by scientists from the National Institute of Agronomic Research in Dijon France.

One of the more important benefits of rosemary is its ability to remove excess oestrogen from the body. Oestrogen is a hormone that contributes to some forms of breast cancer. There are many pharmaceutical drugs that help to reduce this hormone but all have toxic side effects. According to a study done by Dr Zhu at the State University of New Jersey taking a 2% concentration of rosemary extract for 3 weeks significantly inactivates excess oestrogen in the body so this could potentially be a viable substitute for more toxic methods to preventing this type of cancer.

Culinary Uses

The pungent taste of Rosemary goes well with meats potatoes and bread. It is also great for marinades and soups and goes well with other herbs. Rosemary should be used sparingly though as its powerful taste can easily overpower other flavors and take over any dish.

In ancient times, Rosemary was used to mask the smell and flavor of older meats partly because the compounds it contains have antibacterial properties that would kill off the bacteria and partly because the flavor is so strong that would help make the meat taste better. It goes particularly good with lamb and is used in many lamb recipes.

To use rosemary in cooking, strip the needlelike leaves from the branch by pulling them in the opposite direction of which they grow. You want to chop the leaves up and use them sparingly. The stem does have some flavor too, but it is kind of tough so you probably don't want use it in your cooking.

You can buy fresh rosemary in most grocery stores today and you can also get it dry, either with whole leaves or ground up. The ground rosemary loses its potency pretty quickly though, so I recommend you buy fresh in order to get the best taste and health benefits.

You can dry your own rosemary by hanging 4 inch sprigs upside down until they dry.

Lemon Rosemary Salmon

Ingredients:

- 8 springs rosemary
- 1 lemon, sliced thin
- 2 tablespoons olive oil
- 2 salmon fillets
- Salt and pepper to taste

Preparation:

Preheat oven to 400F.

Brush the salmon fillets with olive oil.

Sprinkle salt and pepper on both sides of salmon.

Spread lemon slices in a baking dish in single layer.

Layer 4 sprigs of rosemary on top of lemon

Layer salmon on top of rosemary

Layer 4 remaining sprigs on top of salmon.

Bake 20 minutes or until fish is opaque and flakes with a fork.

Rosemary Roasted Chicken

Ingredients:

- 1 whole chicken
- Salt and pepper to taste
- 1/4 cup chopped rosemary
- 1 small onion, cut into 8 pieces

Preparation:

Preheat oven to 350F.

Season chicken with salt and pepper.

Stuff the chicken with the onion and rosemary.

Roast chicken in oven until cooked through - about 2 1/2 hours.

RED (CAYENNE) PEPPER

Plant Family: Nightshade (Solanaceae)

Where Grown: Originating in South America, it is grown in India, East Africa, Mexico, U.S. China and most tropical regions.

Parts Used: Fruit

Other Names: Cayenne Pepper, Bird Chili, Birds Beak, Mad pepper

Chili peppers have been cultivated since prehistoric times and were popular in South America first as a decorative item and then as food and medicine. In the 15th century Columbus discovered them on his exploration of the Caribbean islands and introduced them to Europe.

They have long been used for their many medicinal properties and even mentioned by Nicholas Culpepper in his 17th century book *"Complete Herbal"* In fact, cayenne pepper is thought by some to be one of the biggest health secrets today and has been studied for its use as a pain reliever as well as its cardiovascular benefits.

Cayenne or red pepper is the finely ground pepper from the seeds and pods of the chili pepper. It is made from the ripened fruit and is a bright red in color. Although it has a mild aroma, is extremely spicy - one of the hottest spices used in cooking.

The peppers grow on a dense shrub with white flowers which grows to be about 2 feet tall. It is propagated from seed in nurseries and does best in warm climates although some do grow it in their home gardens in cooler areas.

Health Benefits

Cayenne pepper has been studied for its health benefits which mostly come from the abundance of capsaicin present in the spice. Capsaicin has been shown to inhibit a hormone that is involved in inflammation (substance P) and, as such, can help reduce inflammation and the pain associated with it. Certain studies have shown that the capsaicin found in cayenne pepper can help with the pain from arthritis, psoriasis and diabetic neuropathy when applied topically.

Cayenne pepper has been historically used to treat circulatory system problems and recent studies show that it has quite a few heart health benefits not the least of which is reducing cholesterol in the blood as well as lowering triglyceride levels. It can also reduce platelet aggregation, thus, reducing blood clotting. It has been shown that cultures that eat a lot of cayenne pepper have a low rate of cardiovascular disease.

Although many people use cayenne pepper on their food because they like the taste, it also has the added benefit of having thermogenic effects that can increase your metabolism for more than 20 min. after eating it which can help with weight loss.

Another benefit of capsaicin is that it helps to break up mucus and, in fact, has compounds that are similar to those found in many over the counter cold remedies. Interestingly enough, cayenne pepper actually works faster than these remedies and with no ill side effects.

You wouldn't think that a spicy pepper could help heal ulcers because you've probably heard that spicy food aggravates them, but the fact is that red pepper can kill the bacteria that cause ulcers as well as stimulate the stomach to make protective juices that prevent ulcers from forming. In addition to that eating red pepper can help heal your gallbladder as well as shrink hemorrhoids.

Like most herbs and spices, red pepper has an abundance of vitamins and minerals and is a powerful antioxidant. It's loaded with Vitamin A, Vitamin C, Vitamin E, Vitamin B6, beta-carotene, Vitamin K, manganese and fiber.

Culinary Uses

Red pepper can be used as a spice in cooking and also as a condiment. You might consider keeping it on the table next to your salt and pepper so you can sprinkle it on your food as it can add zest to almost any dish.

It is used liberally in Mexican cooking and a frequent ingredient in Indian dishes and curries. Western cooking often includes it in egg dishes or added to cheese.

The truth is, that it can go good with any dish and can be delicious added to grilled, roasted or fried meats, salads, soups and stews. It can even be a great addition to spice up your mayonnaise and marinades and it adds a nice spicy surprise when sprinkled in your hot chocolate.

Red pepper does deteriorate rapidly so you want to buy it in small amounts and use it quickly. Store in a dark container because sunlight will cause it to lose potency even faster.

Spicy Chocolate Cookies

Ingredients:

- 1 cup sugar
- 1 cup brown sugar
- 1 cup butter
- 2 eggs
- 1 teaspoon cayenne pepper
- 1 cup cocoa powder
- 2 cups flour
- 1 teaspoon baking powder
- 1/2 teaspoon salt
- 3/4 cup chocolate chips

Preparation:

Preheat oven to 350F.

Cream butter, white sugar and brown sugar until fluffy.

Add eggs to the sugar mixture until well blended.

Whisk the cayenne, baking soda, cocoa and salt together until well blended. Add to the sugar mixture and mix well.

Add flour and mix well.

Fold in the chocolate chips.

Refrigerate for at least 1 hour.

Drop by teaspoonful onto greased cookie sheets.

Bake 10 - 12 minutes.

Sweet And Spicy Chicken Wings

Ingredients:

• 2 pounds chicken wings (you can use breast and legs too
if you want)
• 1 cup maple syrup
• 2 teaspoons cayenne pepper
• 1/3 cup teriyaki sauce
• Olive oil
• Salt

Preparation:

Preheat oven to 350F.

Cut the chicken wings into 3 sections.

Place wings in a baking dish.

Combine the remaining ingredients.

Pour over wings and toss to coat.

Bake for 1 hour or until chicken is fully cooked.

SAFFRON

Plant Family: Iris (Iridaceae)

Where Grown: Originating in Asia, you can now find it being grown in India, Mexico, Spain and Iran

Parts Used: Flower Stigmas

Saffron is by far the most expensive spice and it's no wonder since each little strand is the stigma of a crocus flower, hand picked and harvested - it takes 50,000 flowers to make 1 pound of saffron!

Luckily, this herb is so potent that you really only need a pinch to add flavor to your cooking so it won't cost a kings ransom to add Saffron to your list of kitchen spices and herbs.

The use of saffron dates back to the 7th century and has been documented in the treatment of over 90 illnesses in the span of 4000 years. In ancient times, saffron was woven into textiles, used in rituals, included in dyes, body washes and perfumes and, of course, used as medicine.

Ancient Romans used it to perfume their baths, French ladies of the court used it to tint their hair and German dealers caught adulterating it were burned at the steak.

Today it is still a coveted spice and you do need to be careful when buying it to insure you get pure saffron as it is adulterated still (although I don't think anyone is burned at the steak anymore for doing it!). Pure saffron will be bright red threads with lighter red-orange tips. When submersed in water or milk, they should not impart their red color right away (should take 10 or 15 minutes) as this would be a sign that they have been dyed and may be fake.

Health Benefits

Traditionally used to treat over 90 illnesses, Saffron has wide ranging health benefits. It is said to help treat stomach aches, kidney stones, liver problems, bladder problems, asthma, menstrual problems, depression, insomnia and even baldness. Like many herbs it is beneficial to your heart health because it can also help to lower cholesterol, improve circulation and lower triglycerides.

The carotenoids in saffron are what is responsible for many of the health benefits which include improving skin problems, arthritis and eye health. Recent studies have shown that saffron can be helpful in age-related eye problems and, in fact, in one study every participant that took it saw improved eye health. Saffron has shown promise in helping to reduce cataracts as well as slowing down macular degeneration.

Saffron also includes crocin which is been shown to help with learning and memory retention. Early studies show that it has promise in helping age-related mental decline. Crocin and safranel are also helpful in boosting your immune system and can accelerate the levels of enzymes that help your body find toxins and eliminate them.

In addition to that, saffron can be a good blood purifier and has anti-inflammatory properties that can help relieve joint pain and speed up the healing of burns and cuts. It has also been traditionally used to relieve gastrointestinal problems and help with digestion.

Culinary Uses

Saffron adds an exotic air to any dish and it also helps improve digestion and boost the appetite. Applying heat releases the powerful saffron flavor so it should be steeped in hot water or broth first. You can also toast saffron over low heat to impart the flavor.

Saffron is good in seafood dishes and probably best known for its use in paella. It is also great for risotto and rice dishes and is excellent when added to a marinade for fish. Saffron can also be used to add an interesting flair to breads and cakes.

A little bit of saffron goes a long way and the flavor will intensify the next day so if you are making a dish to have left overs keep this in mind.

Always buy fresh saffron threads, or if you buy ground saffron, make sure you just buy a small amount and use it within 6 months. Be wary of powdered saffron as it is often cut with turmeric or additives and may not be pure saffron.

To store saffron, wrap the threads in tin foil and store in a jar with a tight fitting lid - they will keep for 3 years before flavor starts to diminish.

Paella

Ingredients:

- 3 tablespoons olive oil
- 3 cloves garlic, crushed
- 1 green bell pepper
- 1 red bell pepper
- 1 medium onion, chopped
- 3/4 pound large shrimp, peeled and deveined
- 12 mussels
- 10 ounces spicy turkey sausage links
- 1/2 cup frozen peas
- 4 cups reduced sodium chicken broth
- 1 teaspoon saffron threads
- 4 springs fresh thyme
- 1 bay leaf
- 2 cups white rice
- Salt and pepper to taste
- 1/4 cup chopped parsley

Preparation:

Heat a large skillet on medium and add 2 tablespoons of the olive oil, garlic and rice. Sauté for 3 minutes then add saffron, thyme, bay leaf and chicken broth. Bring to a boil, cover pan and reduce heat to simmer.

In another skillet, add the rest of the olive oil and heat over medium high heat. Add turkey sausage, peppers and onions. Season with salt and pepper and cook until sausage and peppers are cooked thoroughly.

Once the rice pan has been simmering for about 15 minutes, add mussels, shrimp and peas and cover the pan again, let cook for 5 minutes. After 5 minutes remove any unopened mussels as well as the thyme and bay leaf stems.

Combine the chicken and peppers with the rice mixture, top with parsley and serve!

Saffron Rice

Ingredients:

- 2 cups basmati rice
- 3 1/2 cups chicken stock
- 1 tablespoon dried onion
- 1 clove garlic, minced
- 1/2 teaspoon turmeric
- 1/2 teaspoon salt
- 1/2 teaspoon saffron threads, crushed

Preparation

Add ingredients into medium sized pan, stir and bring to a boil. Cover and reduce heat.

Simmer for 15 minutes or until most of the liquid is gone. Cover and remove from heat.

Rice will still steam inside the pot and will stay warm for around an hour. When you are ready to serve, drain any remaining water and fluff up the rice with a fork.

SAGE

Plant Family: Mint (Lamiaceae)

Where Grown: Originating in Northern Europe it is grown all over the Northern Hemisphere with Croatia being the largest producer

Parts Used: Leaves

With hints of both sweet and savory, the peppery taste of sage is most often recognized in stuffing but it can be used in a variety of dishes. It has been used since ancient times as a medicinal, culinary and ornamental herb.

This perennial evergreen plant with blue or purple flowers grows to be about 2 feet tall. The leaves are what is used for both healing and cooking and they are grayish green with soft short hairs on the underside that make them look almost white.

Sage has a long history and was used in ancient times for warding off evil, treating snakebites and increasing fertility in women. Pliny the Elder used it as a diuretic an anesthetic for the skin and a styptic. Charlemagne recommended it for cultivation in the middle Ages and it was very popular then and even used in a blend of spices that was said to ward off the plague.

Ancient Romans considered sage a sacred herb and even had special ceremonies for gathering it and, along with the ancient Greeks, used it to preserve meat. Modern science reveals sage to have potent antioxidant properties which would help retard the spoilage of meat so it looks like the ancient Romans and Greeks were onto something even though they didn't have the benefit of science to back it up.

Today, sage shows promise for a variety of health problems and is used in cuisines around the globe.

Health Benefits

Sage is known as an antibiotic, astringent, antispasmodic, estrogenic and an overall tonic for good health. It contains many volatile oils and flavonoids that contribute to its health properties. The rosmarinic acid in sage is known to be a powerful anti-inflammatory, so eating sage can help reduce inflammation throughout the body. It is recommended for people with asthma, rheumatoid arthritis and other inflammatory conditions.

Sage also has important antioxidant capabilities. In fact, the combination of compounds found in this herb, make it one of the best herbs for preventing oxygen-based damage in the body.

Sage also may have important uses in helping age-related memory problems. In a double-blind, placebo-controlled trial, sage essential oil was found to be effective in managing mild to moderate Alzheimer's disease. Another study in the June 2003 issue of *"Pharmacological Biochemical Behavior"* found that immediate memory recall was improved by using sage essential oil.

Sage may also have benefits in treating diabetes according to a study done at the University of Minho in Braga Portugal in 2006 which focused on studying the anti diabetic effects of a sage tea infusion in mice. It was shown that the sage tea infusion did lower blood glucose levels and, therefore, may be helpful in preventing type II diabetes.

Evidence suggests that sage may also be helpful in relieving menopausal symptoms such as night sweats and hot flashes.

Culinary Uses

Sage can be purchased fresh or dried but the fresh has superior flavor. It can be stored wrapped in a damp paper towel in a plastic bag for a couple of days in the refrigerator. The leaves can be frozen for 2 months. Dried sage will keep for about 6 months.

Unlike many herbs, sage can withstand a long cooking time and is actually better if added at the beginning of the cooking process. This makes it perfect to add into soups and stews but don't limit yourself to those as it really goes with many different foods.

When dry it can taste a little bitter so fresh is always recommended but either way it's strong flavor can overwhelm recipes so use it sparingly. Sage can be used in just about any dish and goes particularly well with Italian dishes like pasta and pizza. It works pretty good with cheeses and makes a tasty addition to breads or biscuits.

Slow Cooker Pork And Apples

Ingredients:

- 4 large granny smith apples, cored and cut
- 3 - 4 pound boneless pork roast
- 1/3 cup apple juice
- 1 teaspoon salt
- 1/2 teaspoon black pepper
- 1 large onion cut into 8ths
- 1 sprig fresh sage
- 1 sprig fresh rosemary

Preparation:

Rub roast with salt and pepper and brown under broiler or in a skillet rubbed with olive oil.

Place apple pieces on bottom of crock pot, add roast and pour apple juice over it.

Place onions on top of roast, sprinkle sage and rosemary on top of onions.

Cool on low for 7 - 8 hours. Roast should be 155 degrees F when done.

Sage Biscuits

Ingredients:

- 2 cups flour
- 6 tablespoons butter, chilled and diced (unsalted)
- 1/2 teaspoon baking soda
- 2 teaspoons baking powder
- 1 teaspoon salt
- 1/4 cup sage leaves, chopped
- 3/4 cup buttermilk

Preparation:

Preheat over to 450F

Sift flour, baking soda, baking powder and salt.

Cut the butter into the flour mixture. Mix until it is like course sand.

Mix in sage.

Add buttermilk until the flour mix is just moist - add gradually as you may not need as much or if you need more than specific above, add it.

Make a ball with the dough and roll until 1/2" thick and cut into squares (alternatively you could break off biscuit sized pieces of the dough).

Bake on cookie sheet about 12 minutes.

SAVORY

Plant Family: Mint (Lamiaceae)

Where Grown: Throughout Europe, Mediterranean and North Africa

Parts Used: Leaves

Other Names: Bean Herb, Donkey Pepper, Pepperherb

The herb savory has 2 varieties, summer and winter. The summer variety is actually preferred for culinary use as it is more tender and delicate in flavor. Savory has been described as part herb and part spice with a flavor reminiscent of thyme but with a peppery bite.

Summer savory is an annual with slender branches and a delicate flavor. It grows to about 18 inches tall. Winter savory is a short shrub-like perennial that grows only 12 inches in height. Both varieties have light pink or purple flowers that attract bees to your garden.

Savory is traditionally used in Italian cuisine especially with beans and it was very popular with the ancient Romans who used it mixed in vinegar as a condiment on the table.

In ancient times, savory was mixed with ground-up garbanzo beans and water and then baked into a flat cracker. This was actually a pretty popular snack back in the day. Today, savory can be used in a variety of dishes and also has many health benefits.

Health Benefits

Savory, as an herb, is used as a general tonic for digestion. It is also a powerful anti-septic and used in toothpaste and soap even today.

It's been used since ancient times for its health benefits which have included the ability to treat bee stings, soothe stomachaches and relieve flatulence. It was also reputed to promote health of the female reproductive system and was even used as an aphrodisiac.

Culinary Uses

As discussed above, savory goes really great with all kinds of beans and it is also very commonly used as a seasoning for green vegetables.

The summer savory goes perfect with green beans and the winter savory is better used for lentils and dried beans.

Summer savory can be eaten fresh and raw and added to salads or as a garnish but winter savory should always be cooked as it is rather tough and the flavor will come out better after cooking.

Savory Green Beans

Ingredients:

- 1 pound fresh green beans, trimmed and cut
- 1 tablespoon olive oil
- 1 clove garlic, minced
- 1/2 cup water
- 2 tablespoons fresh summer savory, minced
- 1/2 teaspoon salt

Ingredients:

Sauté garlic in olive oil in a large skillet until tender.

Add green beans, water, savory and salt.

Bring to boil, reduce heat, cover and simmer for about 10 minutes until beans are tender.

Savory Broiled Salmon

Ingredients:

- 2 pounds salmon fillet
- 1/2 cup lemon juice
- 2 cloves garlic, pressed
- 1 tablespoon savory

Ingredients:

Combine lemon juice, savory and garlic in a small saucepan and heat until steaming. Remove from heat and cool thoroughly.

Once the marinade is cool, arrange salmon in a shallow dish and pour marinade over it. Cover and put in the refrigerator for 2 hours.

Broil salmon until it flakes easily - about 4 minutes each side.

TAMARIND

Plant Family: Bean (Fabaceae)

Where Grown: East Africa, Asia, Mexico

Parts Used: Pulp From The Pods

Tamarind comes from the pulp of a bean pod that grows on a tree. This tree is indigenous to tropical Africa and is now cultivated in other tropical areas. It grows to be about 50 feet tall and yields legumes that have a brown outer coating and gooey pulp with seeds inside.

The taste of tamarind can be best described as tart, especially before it has ripened properly. It is a favorite in sweet and sour dishes and as the pod matures, the sugars develop adding sweetness into the acidic sourness of the pulp.

In the tropics, you can buy tamarind pods in the spring and summer, but in the West we mostly by it as a paste or in blocks. Tamarind is a key ingredient in many cuisines and can be found in curries, chutneys and, believe it or not, Worcestershire sauce.

Health Benefits

Tamarind has long been used to cure many ailments. It is said to help get rid of intestinal parasites, soothe fevers, relieve liver problems and help with bile disorders as well as gallbladder problems. Tamarind extract is even used in some solutions to treat dry eyes.

Tamarind pulp has a lot of fiber which is why it's often used to treat constipation. In fact, 100 g of the pulp has over 13% of dietary fiber which not only helps with constipation but it also binds to toxins which can help protect your colon from exposure to toxic chemicals. It also binds to bile salts which can help lower your levels of LDL cholesterol because it prevents reabsorption of these salts back into the body.

Tamarind is also used to help treat fevers and colds and contains compounds that help kill bacteria. It is said that gargling with it can help treat sore throats and it can also be used to help with vomiting, flatulence and indigestion.

The leaves of the tree when ground into a poultice and applied topically can help treat burns and inflamed joints.

Studies on animals have shown that tamarind may have a role in helping to lower serum cholesterol as well as blood sugar levels.

Tamarind is loaded with healthy vitamins and minerals including Vitamin C, Vitamin A, calcium, iron, phosphorus, carotene, riboflavin, niacin, copper, potassium, magnesium, selenium, and folic acid.

Culinary Uses

For cooking, it is the flesh inside the pod that is used. You'll find it in jams, chutneys, hot and sour soups and curries and sometimes even eaten dried, salted or candied. In Egypt it is used in a sour, chilled drink and it is a popular ingredient in Middle Eastern, Indian, Southeast Asian and Thai foods.

You can buy fresh pods in late spring and early summer but most of the tamarind found in the West is processed into paste or sold in a compressed block. To use it, break some off the block and soak it in water then strain to remove pulp and seeds and use as directed.

Tamarind Chutney

Ingredients:

- 2 cups tamarind pulp
- 2 tablespoons sugar
- 1 teaspoon red chili powder
- 1 teaspoon cumin
- 1/2 cup water
- Salt to taste

Preparation:

In a small saucepan, boil ingredients until you get a ketchup like consistency.

(Note: if you buy block tamarind, then you will need to soak it in water and squeeze out the pulp).

TARRAGON

Plant Family: Daisy (Asteraceae)

Where Grown: Central and Southern Europe, Mexico

Parts Used: Leaves

Other Names: Dragon Herb

Perhaps most popular in French cuisine, tarragon provides the palate with a medley of tastes from a peppery anise to savory lavender all in the same bite. It is originally from the Baltic area and is now used in pretty much every cuisine around the globe.

Tarragon is a perennial that grows to about 2 feet in height with slender branches that have long been glossy green leaves and yellow flowers. It is best cultivated by root division as the seeds almost always are sterile.

Thought to be brought to Europe by invading Mongols in the 13th century, tarragon was cooked as a vegetable in ancient times and was thought to be able to cure snakebites. The ancient Greeks chewed it to help relieve toothache pain.

Garden pests don't like the taste of tarragon so it is a good companion plant to have in a garden that will help keep away insects that can harm your other plants.

Health Benefits

Like many herbs, tarragon has a long list of ills that it has been traditionally used to treat. It is said to be a digestive aid and mild sedative and can also help relieve menstrual cramps, insomnia, intestinal worms, loss of appetite, depression, hyperactivity and, when combined with fennel, can be a good natural laxative to relieve constipation.

Tarragon is said to promote the production of bile and help eliminate waste. It contains eugenol which is an anesthetic and pain reliever, so chewing the leaves actually can relieve toothache pain. When crushed and applied to the skin the leaves can also help treat rashes and other skin irritations.

Tarragon is a great source of iron, calcium and manganese and it also contains potassium, Vitamin A, magnesium, copper, zinc and phosphorus.

Culinary Uses

Tarragon is one of the 4 fine herbs of French cooking and probably best known for its use in béarnaise sauce. The flavor of the herb is much more intense when fresh and you can freeze whole sprigs for 3 to 5 months.

Tarragon is often used in vinegar as a flavoring and vinegar also helps preserve the herb. You'll often find it as an ingredient in pickles and relishes. It can also be used in infused oils to add flavor.

Tarragon goes well with a lot of foods and you often see it paired with chicken and seafood but it can also be effective in egg and cheese dishes, soups and fresh fruit cups. It makes a great basting sauce when combined with butter lemon and chives.

Tarragon Tomato Shrimp

Ingredients:

- 2 pounds fresh shrimp, peeled and deveined
- 2 tablespoons olive oil
- 2 cloves garlic, minced
- 1 cup fresh tomatoes, chopped
- 1 tablespoon fresh tarragon, minced
- 1/2 teaspoon salt
- 1/4 teaspoon butter

Preparation:

In a large pan, cook shrimp and garlic in olive oil for 2 minutes.

Stir in the rest of the ingredients.

Cook until shrimp are opaque pink (about 4 or 5 minutes)

Tarragon Cranberry Chicken Salad

Ingredients:

- Cooked Chicken Breast chopped to make 2 cups
- 2 teaspoons fresh tarragon, chopped
- 1/4 cup dried cranberries, chopped in to small pieces
- 1/4 up mayonnaise
- 1 celery stalk including leaves, chopped fine
- Salt and pepper to taste

Preparation:

Mix everything together and serve on bread or on a bed of lettuce. You can chop the chicken into large chunks if you prefer, or smaller pieces which is how I like it. This is a great way to add zip to an everyday dish!

THYME

Plant Family: Mint (Lamiaceae)

Where Grown: Originating in Southern Europe, it is cultivated in all of Europe, Africa and North America

Parts Used: Leaves

One of the oldest herbs, thyme has over 60 different varieties including lemon thyme, orange time and hyssop thyme, all with a slightly different flavor. This perennial plant is easy to grow in home gardens and can be propagated by seeds, cuttings or dividing root sections.

Thyme is a bushy aromatic perennial evergreen shrub that has small grayish green leaves and flowers that range from pale pink to purple.

It has been used since ancient times; the Egyptians used thyme for embalming, the ancient Greeks used it for incense and in their baths and the Romans used it to purify their rooms. It's said to be a source of courage and in medieval times women gave knights gifts that included sprigs of thyme. It was thought that if you placed thyme under your pillow it could ward off nightmares.

Much as we humans love the smell of thyme, insects are repelled by it, so you can make a good natural insect repellent by steeping thyme in hot water and then putting that into a spray bottle and spraying it around your windows and doors or wherever you don't want insects coming into the house. Bees do love the plant though and honey made from pollen gathered from thyme flowers is quite delicious.

Health Benefits

The main oil in thyme is thymol which is an antiseptic and the active ingredient in common products such as Listerine mouthwash and Vicks vapor rub as well as some all natural hand sanitizers. It was once used to medicate bandages and is reputed to be an effective remedy for toenail fungus.

Thyme has a long history in treating respiratory problems. Recent studies show the volatile oils in thyme are what make it effective for this. Thyme tea can be used for bronchitis and coughs. Respiratory problems can be treated by a tincture of essential oils, tea or by steam inhalation.

These volatile oils also have antimicrobial activity that help protect against bacteria and fungus. Thyme has long been used to preserve and decontaminate food. In fact the Feb 2004 issue of *"Food Microbiology"* revealed research that showed that thyme essential oil could decontaminate lettuce inoculated with Shigella an infectious organism that causes diarrhea and may cause intestinal damage.

Thyme also helps the body digest fatty foods so it's great to include it in fatty dishes.

Thyme has lots of vitamins and minerals; in fact it is loaded with Vitamin K and also has Vitamin A, Vitamin C, iron, manganese, calcium, dietary fiber, tryptophan and various flavonoids making it a great antioxidant herb.

Culinary Uses

Thyme is a basic herb in most cuisines and is used to flavor meats, stews and soups. It goes particularly well with lamb. Thyme blends well with other spices and is a common component in herbes de provence as well as bouquet garni.

Thyme can be used both fresh and dried but the fresh will have more flavor. That being said, dried thyme does retain its flavor more than most other dried herbs. If you are substituting in a recipe use one third as much dried as fresh but try to use fresh herbs whenever possible.

When using fresh thyme, you want to strip the leaves off the stems and add it early in the cooking process because thyme slowly releases its flavors.

Thyme tends to go best with earthy types of foods such as game meats, root vegetables and mushrooms.

Lemon Thyme Rice

Ingredients:

- 3/4 cup basmati or jasmati rice
- 1 tablespoon fresh thyme, chopped fine
- Juice from 1/2 lemon (about 1 tablespoon)
- 1 1/2 cup water
- Salt and pepper to taste

Preparation:

Boil water in a medium pot, add a pinch of salt and the rice. Bring to boil, and then reduce heat to low.

Add thyme and lemon juice. Stir and simmer until rice is cooked (about 25 minutes). Season with salt and pepper to taste.

Roasted Vegetables And Fresh Thyme

Ingredients:

- 2 pounds carrots, peeled
- 2 pounds parsnips, peeled
- 2 pounds sweet potato, peeled
- 1/4 cup olive oil
- 1 tablespoon salt
- 1/2 tablespoon fresh black pepper
- 2 tablespoons fresh thyme, crushed and chopped
- 2 tablespoons parsley, chopped fine
- 2 oz balsamic vinegar

Preparation:

Preheat over to 375F.

Cut the vegetables into 2" chunks.

Put vegetables in a large bowl and cover with olive oil, salt and pepper. Stir to coat.

Lay vegetables in a single layer on a baking sheet (you might need more than 1 baking sheet).

Bake for about 30 minutes to an hour until vegetables are soft. The sweet potato might take longer so you might put it in 15 minutes before the others, or leave it to cook after you take the others out.

Let vegetables cool a bit then put them all in a large bowl, drizzle with balsamic vinegar, thyme and parsley then mix to coat. Add salt and pepper to taste.

TURMERIC

Plant Family: Ginger (Zingiberaceae)

Where Grown: Originating in Eastern Asia and grown extensively in India

Parts Used: Root

Other Names: Indian Saffron

Turmeric is perhaps the healthiest of all the spices and has been used throughout history as a food flavoring, health remedy and dye. It is native to tropical South Asia and is actually the root of the curcuma longa plant. The earthy, mustardy ginger flavor of turmeric is most closely associated with curry.

Turmeric itself is a rhizome or root. It is the underground stem of the plant that grows into woody bulbous fingers much like ginger. The root is boiled and then dried and ground into powder. While it can be used in its natural form in areas where it is grown, the rest of the world mostly uses it in powdered form.

The plant itself is a perennial that grows to be about 5 or 6 feet tall and has trumpet shaped yellow flowers. It only grows in the tropics so you won't find it in many home gardens. The dried root is too hard for grinding at home anyway and needs to be done commercially.

Turmeric has long been used for a variety of health remedies and is even so revered that has been used in ceremonies in India and still is to this day.

Commonly used in curries, turmeric is known for its persistent yellow color which stains just about everything it comes in contact with. It is often used as a dye and is also used to color many of the common foods we eat every day including regular yellow hotdog mustard.

Health Benefits

While the medicinal benefits of turmeric have been known since ancient times, recent studies actually prove that this is not just folklore.

Turmeric is popular in ancient Chinese and Indian health systems and has long been used for its powerful anti-inflammatory properties. Traditionally it has been used to treat a variety of ailments including chest pain, toothache, jaundice, menstrual problems, flatulence and colic.

The healing component in turmeric is called curcumin which is currently being studied for its possible benefits in treating Alzheimer's and cancer. There are 61 clinical trials registered in the United States to study the use of dietary curcumin and its effect on a variety of clinical disorders.

Curcumin is also what gives turmeric its yellow color as well as its anti-inflammatory properties. It is said that the anti-inflammatory effects of curcumin can be compared to pharmaceuticals like hydrocortisone and phenylbutazone as well as over the counter drugs but curcumin does not have the toxic side effects that these drugs have.

A study done on mice shows that curcumin may have promise in treating inflammatory bowel diseases like ulcerative colitis and Crohn's disease. Other clinical studies show that turmeric may provide relief for rheumatoid arthritis sufferers due to its anti-inflammatory and antioxidant properties.

Another animal study published in April 2004 suggests that curcumin may be able to correct the most common expression of the genetic defect responsible for cystic fibrosis.

Curcumin is also being studied for cancer prevention. The antioxidant actions help protect cells from free radical damage, especially colon cells which replicate quite quickly. Epidemiological studies have linked the frequent use of turmeric to lower rates of many types of cancers including breast, lung, prostate and colon. Laboratory tests show that it can help prevent tumors from forming. A study at the University of Texas suggest that it may help slow the spreading of breast cancer cells to the lungs in mice. Another study done at University of Texas and published in *Biochemical Pharmacology* showed that curcumin inhibits the activation of a molecule that signals genes to produce molecules that promote cancer cell growth.

Turmeric may also have a role in cardiovascular health because it prevents the oxidation of cholesterol - the process which is attributed to plaque buildup in the arteries. It can also help keep homocysteine levels down.

In addition to that, turmeric also stimulates the gallbladder which may help improve digestion.

Turmeric has anti fungal and antibacterial properties and test tube and animal studies show it may be effective in killing bacteria and viruses.

Turmeric has lots of vitamins and minerals such as manganese, iron, vitamin B6, dietary fiber and potassium

Please note that there is some suggestion that the health benefits of turmeric will only be seen if you use it in conjunction with black pepper but since most dishes also have black pepper this shouldn't be a problem!

Although typically safe in food doses, turmeric might interfere with blood thinning medication, drugs that reduce stomach acid and diabetes medications so you will want to consult your doctor first if you are considering adding foods with turmeric to your diet.

Culinary Uses

Turmeric is a key ingredient in Indian, Thai and Persian dishes where you will often find it in curries and mustard pickles. It goes good with rice, vegetables, chicken, turkey and is great when used in dressings. It is very pungent and gets stronger during cooking. As noted above, the yellow dye is very powerful so you want to avoid getting it on your clothes and hands during the cooking process.

Turmeric is highly susceptible to light so you want to store in a cool, dry and dark place.

Broccoli Chicken Stir Fry

Ingredients:

- 1 pound chicken breast, cut into strips or bite size chunks
- 4 cups broccoli, cut up into bite size chunks
- 4 cloves garlic, pressed
- 2" ginger root, pressed
- 1 onion, chopped
- 1 tablespoon turmeric
- 2 tablespoons coconut oil (or butter)

Preparation:

In a large pan or wok, sauté the onions in the oil or butter until they are soft.

Add ginger and garlic and cook for 1 minute.

Stir in turmeric and cook for another minute.

Add chicken and broccoli. Cook until chicken is cooked through, stirring occasionally.

Serve with fresh ground black pepper in order to experience all the health benefits!

Note: try not to get too much of the turmeric on your fingers as it will turn them yellow for quite some time. It will also stain your clothes, cutting board, kitchen towels and anything else it comes in contact with!

Roasted Butternut Squash with Turmeric

Ingredients:

- 1 butternut squash peeled and cut into chunks
- 1 teaspoon turmeric
- 1/2 teaspoon fresh ground black pepper
- 1 tablespoons coconut oil

Preparation:

Preheat oven to 350F.

In a large bowl, combine all the ingredients. Toss to coat all sides of the squash chunks. (Don't use your hand to toss unless you want yellow hands for the next couple of days! You can put on food gloves or use a really long spoon).

Spread the chunks out on a baking sheet and roast for 45 minutes or until the squash is soft.

VANILLA BEAN

Plant Family: Orchid (Orchidaceae)

Where Grown: Originating in South America, it is now also grown in Tahiti, Central Africa, Madagascar, Mexico and Central America

Parts Used: Bean Pods and Seeds

Vanilla bean is an ancient aromatic spice that didn't make its debut in the New World until the 16th century because it could only grow in the tropical regions of South America. It was the Totonaca Indians of Mexico that first discovered this bean which they then surrendered to the Aztecs after they were conquered. Later on, Spanish explorers conquered the Aztecs and brought the tasty spice back to Europe.

The spice that we know of as vanilla actually comes from the bean of an orchid plant that grows on the tlilxochitl vine and needs to be hand pollinated when not grown in its original location because it can only be naturally pollinated by a specific species of bee that lives only in Mexico.

Needless to say, the rest of the world loved the spice so much that they felt that hand pollinating wasn't really too much work and it is now cultivated in many tropical countries. Of course, this does make the spice very expensive and it is one of the most costly second only to saffron.

Vanilla is actually one of the most loved flavors with a complex floral bouquet that is used extensively in baking as well as in aromatherapy, perfumes, skin care products and soaps.

Interestingly enough, the pod isn't really that tasty while growing on the vine but once it is harvested and goes through a drying process it becomes quite flavorful. It is actually the seeds inside the pod that hold the most vanillin, the compound responsible for the flavor and aroma.

Health Benefits

Vanilla was traditionally used as an aphrodisiac and remedy for fever but modern studies show it may have more medicinal uses than that.

In vitro tests show it might have uses in stopping the growth of bacteria - a study published in *"Journal of Food Protection"*in 2005 tested the effect of vanillin on bacteria and it was shown to inhibit the growth of certain types of bacteria.

The antioxidant properties in vanilla may also help fight cancer according to an article published in the *"European Journal of Pharmaceutical Sciences"* in 2005 where vanilla bean extracts tested on animals showed a reduction in the number of breast cancer cells.

Vanilla essential oils are used extensively in aromatherapy and are shown to produce a calming effect so it is useful in treating anxiety is well as being used as an aroma that can help induce relaxation. It is shown to increase the levels of catecholamines in the body and maybe even be considered to be mildly addictive.

Vanilla contains B complex vitamins such as niacin, pantothenic acid, thiamin, riboflavin and Vitamin B6 and has traced amounts of zinc, iron, potassium, calcium, magnesium and manganese.

Culinary Uses

The heady aroma of vanilla makes it a perfect spice to include in baked goods and, indeed, you can find vanilla extract listed as an ingredient on almost every recipe for cookies and cakes. There are 3 ways the spice can be used:

1) The whole pod usually cut open and included in a liquid or the seeds scraped out for baking

2) The extract which is commonly used in many baked goods, and

3) In powder form - which is rarely used but good for anyone wanting vanilla flavor but without the alcohol that is in the liquid vanilla extract.

When buying vanilla extract for your baking, you want to be sure to get pure vanilla. There are a lot of imitation extracts out there and, while they will be a little bit less expensive, they won't taste nearly as good and spending those extra few dollars to get the real thing will be well worth it.

Vanilla Bean Cookies

Ingredients:

- 2 tablespoons Crisco or other vegetable shortening
- 6 tablespoons butter, softened
- 3/4 cup sugar
- 2 vanilla beans
- 1 teaspoon pure vanilla extract
- 1 egg
- 1 1/4 cup flour
- 1/2 teaspoon salt
- 1 teaspoon baking powder

Preparation:

In a large bowl mix together the butter shortening and 3/4 cup of the sugar - blend until light and fluffy.

Slit the vanilla beans lengthwise and scrap seeds into the butter mixture. Add eggs and vanilla extract and mix well.

Sift flour, salt and baking powder into the butter mixture and stir until just combined.

Form dough into a log and wrap in waxed paper. Chill for anywhere from 4 hours to 3 days.

Preheat over to 375F.

Cut log into 1/4" slices for each cookie. Optionally roll the cookies in sugar to coat the tops. Bake for 10 - 12 minutes.

Fruit Salad With Vanilla Bean Syrup

Ingredients:

- 1 vanilla bean
- 1/2 cup water
- 1/3 cup sugar
- 1 cup blueberries
- 1 cup raspberries
- 1 cup strawberries, cored and halved

Preparation:

Split vanilla bean and scrape seeds into a small saucepan. Add water and sugar and stir to mix.

Bring to a boil, reduce heat and simmer, stirring occasionally, until about half the volume is reduced - about 10 minutes.

Let syrup cool.

Arrange fruits in a medium bowl and pour cooled syrup over the top.

Butternut Squash and Vanilla Bean Soup

Ingredients:

- 2 pounds butternut squash, cut in half
- 3 tablespoons olive oil
- 4 cups vegetable stock
- 1 vanilla bean
- 1/2 cup yogurt
- Salt & pepper to taste

Preparation:

Preheat over to 400F.

Drizzle squash with oil and season with salt and pepper. Place on baking sheet and bake until tender when pierced with a fork (about 40 minutes).

Scrape out the seeds, and remove flesh from skin.

Cut the vanilla bean lengthwise with a knife and scrape the seeds into a blender. Add the squash and vegetable stock and blend until creamy - season with more salt and pepper to taste. Add yogurt and blend.

Conclusion

I hope this book gives you a new appreciation of herbs and spices - not just for making food taste better but for improving your health too. I sure would appreciate your review of my book over at Amazon and I do thank you for buying it!

If you want to learn more about how eating delicious food can improve your health and get more healthy recipes, check out the rest of my healing foods books:

Also, I would love to talk to you on my blog, facebook or twitter:

Blog - http://www.healingfoodscookbooks.com

Facebook - http://www.facebook.com/healingfoodsbooks

Twitter - http://www.twitter.com/healingfoodscb

And don't forget to pick up my other books on healthy eating:

Healing Desserts : Guilt Free Desserts Made Healthier With Healing Foods, Herbs and Spices

Anti-Aging Herbs : Top Anti Aging Foods And How To Improve Your Health With Recipes That Use Them

Printed in Great Britain
by Amazon

82671639R00129